CLAWING AT THE LIMITS OF COOL

Miles Davis, John Coltrane, and the
Greatest Jazz Collaboration Ever

CLAWING AT THE LIMITS OF COOL

Farah Jasmine Griffin / Salim Washington

ST. MARTIN'S PRESS
THOMAS DUNNE BOOKS
NEW YORK

THOMAS DUNNE BOOKS.
An imprint of St. Martin's Press.

www.thomasdunnebooks.com
www.stmartins.com

Library of Congress Cataloging-in-Publication Data

Griffin, Farah Jasmine.
    Clawing at the limits of cool : Miles Davis, John Coltrane, and the greatest jazz collaboration ever / Farah Jasmine Griffin, Salim Washington. —1st Thomas Dunne Books ed.
        p. cm.
    Includes bibliographical references (p. 273) and index.
    ISBN-13: 978-0-312-32785-9
    ISBN-10: 0-312-32785-4
    1. Jazz—History and criticism.   2. Davis, Miles.   3. Coltrane, John, 1926–1967.   4. Miles Davis Quintet.   5. Miles Davis Sextet.
I. Washington, Salim.   II. Title.
    ML3508.G75   2008
    781.65'50922—dc22

                                                        2008009313

First Edition: August 2008

10 9 8 7 6 5 4 3 2 1

For Blues People,
especially those who suffered
in the aftermath of Katrina

CONTENTS

CLAWING AT THE LIMITS OF COOL

PRELUDE: THE HEAD

I think it was the beginning of another level of expression in this music.

—RASHIED ALI

FOR MANY, MILES DAVIS AND JOHN COLTRANE were the last major innovators in jazz. Decades after their deaths, their shadows linger over modern music, affecting genres from soul and hip-hop to the experimental wings of European concert music. Within the world of jazz there has been no musician since whose influence runs as wide and as deep. The only artists whose contributions are comparable, in the sense of affecting the way other musicians think and play, are the great pace setters who came before them—Louis Armstrong, Duke Ellington, Charles Parker, Billie Holiday, and a handful of others. And, like these giants, both Davis and Coltrane have become icons far beyond the world of jazz—indeed, beyond the world of music.

In six years, Davis and Coltrane created a band that displayed a perfect mix of form and content, an ensemble that provided an aesthetic model for its time period while also providing artistic answers for the future. The balance between hot and cool playing, between head-spinning innovation and toe-tapping familiarity, the new *feeling* articulated by the band, all spoke to the times and to the necessities of black life in midcentury America.

Both Coltrane and Davis, known to musicians simply as "Trane" and "the Chief," were artists whose approaches to their instruments inspired others not only to imitate their musical ideas, but also to mimic the minutiae of their personal technical mannerisms. These include everything from material changes, such as the widespread use of Harmon mutes for trumpets on ballads or the preponderance of alto and tenor saxophonists who now double on soprano saxophone, to sound production, such as Trane's hard edge or the Chief's squeezed notes, and extend even to styles of melodic ornamentation.

In an art form that reveres the improvisations of outstanding soloists, their ability to create memorable statements places them in select company, and their solos are the normal entry point for appreciating their artistry. However, Trane and the Chief were innovative in other ways as well. They were leading improvisers, yes, but they also have become canonical as composers, bandleaders, and musical thinkers who never rested upon their laurels but continued to invent and try out new ideas. Although this is an impressive array of achievements with expansive implications for American music in general, their musical excellence alone does not exhaust their importance in our culture. Coltrane and Davis have iconic stature in American culture not only for their music, but for the examples they set as men and particularly as black men during one of the most socially dynamic periods in our history.

Both the ways in which they navigated their art form vis-à-vis its artistic and social contexts and the ways in which their personas spoke, and continue to speak, to our culture remain important parts of their legacy.

Miles's public persona, among other things, expresses the confidence and hipness that became so important to American masculinity, and did so in a way that was genuinely cool, virtually free of the predictable affectations of pretenders. The ways in which the Chief spoke and dressed inspired those for whom style mattered. When many of the great bandleaders required their musicians to wear uniforms, or at least suits, in order to be considered presentable, Miles wore richly colored sports coats made of fine fabric, and he expected his band mates to be equally well dressed. He attended to sartorial details such as the type of stitching on his shoes. His personal affect was direct and pointed; there were no gratuitous smiles or any of the pretenses of the entertainer. Miles's manner seemed to say: "The coon show is officially over; we are here to play."

While the Chief was savvy enough to capitalize upon his status, he didn't have to fake the funk. Miles Dewey Davis III was raised to be a confident black genius; sustained achievement had been a matter of course in his family for generations. He came into the world with a long pedigree and surrounded by flesh-and-blood examples of how to maintain dignity and to successfully maneuver the world even in harsh, racist environments. Breaking barriers, superb intellectual achievement, and financial success were all legacies bequeathed to Miles not only by his father's generation, but by his grandfather's as well.

His frank outspokenness, take-no-shit attitude, and self-confidence recalled the courage of politically minded artists like Paul Robeson. But, unlike Robeson—the outspoken actor, athlete, singer, and activist—Miles was consistently able to capture the imagination of generations of black people as well as whites in such a way that his struggles against the unthinking and unhip in our culture were constantly celebrated. (It should be noted that unlike Robeson, Davis was never seen to be a major threat to U.S. capitalism, so he escaped the governmental harassment that haunted Robeson throughout much of his life.)

Saxophonist Carl Grubbs, who was Coltrane's nephew by marriage, recalls of Miles Davis, "We were not trying to be like Pops. Nobody wanted to be that guy sweating with the handkerchief. We wanted to be musicians because of people like Miles. Miles was hip. The music was hot and he was clean, standing there in a suit . . . not even a suit, but a sports jacket. And he would look like this—" (Grubbs strikes a pose where Miles looks askance in an enigmatic way.) Davis biographer Quincy Troupe once admitted to the Chief that he and others in his generation who participated in the protests, sit-ins, and demonstrations of the civil rights movement looked to Miles as a model for how to think and behave under pressure. Troupe's fellow St. Louisian saxophonist Oliver Lake, himself an innovative and stylish musician, recalls, "I wanted to dress like Miles; be cool like Miles."[1]

Even in our own time, through advertising campaigns for products as various as Gap clothing, Hennessy, and Apple computers, we can see Miles Davis's image used as a symbol for innovation and the courage to follow one's conviction. All the ads emphasize Miles's uniqueness as an artist and persona. In the Gap series, he joins James Dean, Chet Baker, Marilyn Monroe, and Steve McQueen—nostalgic icons of a cool sexiness. The Hennessy series features strikingly beautiful African American celebrities such as Pam Grier and Marvin Gaye, with the caption "Never Blend In." The computer ad is part of a 1998 print and television campaign featuring portraits of cultural icons known for brilliance, creativity, originality, and courage; these include Albert Einstein, Bob Dylan, Ted Turner, James Dean, Marilyn Monroe, Pablo Picasso, John Lennon and Yoko Ono, Thomas Edison, the Reverend Martin Luther King Jr., Amelia Earhart, Martha Graham, Maria Callas, and others. The figures are not identified by name; the simple, if ungrammatical caption "Think Different" accompanies each image. According to Allen Olivo, senior director for worldwide marketing communications at Apple, "The premise is that people who use Apple computers are different and that we make computers for those creative people who believe that one person can change the world." By not identifying the figures in the striking black-and-white images, Apple executives also sought to establish their consumers as people in the know, as part of the "cognoscenti."[2]

Although mainstream culture may have taken to flattening out his persona for such ends, the Chief is still revered today among musicians as one of the people whose music and attitude really matter. Saxophonist Lake asserts, "Miles was always stretching . . . that has been an inspiration for me throughout my career: electric Miles, acoustic Miles, straight-ahead Miles, experimenting Miles. . . . The wealth of all his recorded music has been and will be an inspiration to the world."[3]

Likewise, John Coltrane is revered not only for his prodigious musicianship, but also for who he was as a person and for the example he set for anyone in pursuit of mastery at his craft. He stands as a premier example of black creative genius and as a spiritual mentor who brought a decidedly secular music to the realm of the sublime. Once Trane reached his mature stages, it was as if he were dealing directly in spirit matter, with the medium of music serving as a material expression of a higher force. Like his mentor, the Chief, Trane was courageous enough to constantly experiment and grow beyond what he had done before. While Miles, in his changing musical styles, seemed to be exercising his savvy for music and for trendsetting, Trane was clearly on a mission from God. He wanted his music to worship the Creator and to bear witness for his listeners about the beauty of life and creation. While Miles set trends for ways to play the music, Trane consistently risked critical and popular rejection of his music through his relentless expansion and experimentation. His courage and his sheer mastery of the technical rigors of the saxophone changed the way young musicians saw their life's mission; his example inspired generations of musicians to push themselves harder to discover new possibilities through diligence and dedication. Two generations later, saxophonist Joshua Redman would say of Trane's music: "At certain times in my life this music has kind of swept me up and transported me to a place where I can sense that there is something greater than the material existence of things. And a fabric that binds the material world together and offers an escape from that world."[4] For Redman, as for a number of other musicians, the deep spirituality of Trane's music is also evidence of his artistic integrity. In another context, Redman comments:

> *Coltrane, in a certain way, is a paradox, because he is one of the most elusive and one of the most uncompromising artists—one of the purist* [sic] *artists in the history of jazz. You can't get purer than Coltrane. Everything that he did was all about music and all about the artistry and spiritual quest. No concessions were made to commercial issues or even performance issues—issues of audience satisfaction. Yet, at the same time, he is one of the most compelling and in some ways one of the most accessible artists in the history of jazz. . . . I think he was accessible and compelling precisely because he was so uncompromising. The integrity and purity that he had was so apparent to people. You could hear it in the music; you could see it in photographs. It's beautiful and accessible in its intensity, and the sense of resolve and devotion is so visible on his face.*[5]

In addition to musicians, a generation of painters, poets, and activists heard in Trane's music a call to action. The poet Michael Harper tells us Coltrane's energy and passion was "the kind of energy it takes to break oppressive conditions, oppressive musical strictures, and oppressive societal situations."[6] Consequently, for many others like Harper, Trane came to exemplify the revolutionary tenor of the 1960s.

Coltrane, like Davis, was born into a literate, middle-class family that exercised courageous leadership and high achievement. As Trane would put it, his maternal grandfather, Reverend Blair, "was the dominant cat" in his family. Both of his grandfathers, however, were ministers. While Coltrane's religious upbringing was not overly strict, he was not a stranger to the power of God or the notion of sanctified living, and both would prove important to his personal and musical development in later years. Coltrane's father, a tailor who played and sang music for his own enjoyment, was a quiet, humble man. These were traits that John Coltrane embodied as well.

Despite the influence of the male father figures in his life, it was ultimately extraordinary women who raised and nurtured the young Coltrane. His father and grandfather died before his teenage years, so for his entire adolescence and part of his young adulthood he lived with his mother and aunt. The protective environment that these women provided was crucial for his development. From the very beginning, Coltrane was an indefatigable worker at his saxophone, spending hours upon hours practicing every day. He was able to do so long before he was gainfully employed as a musician. And although he worked briefly for the Campbell Soup Company as a young man in Philadelphia, for the most part, the women in his life provided for him in such a way that he could devote himself almost entirely to music.

This, perhaps, is one of the most significant differences in the way that the two men were raised. While Coltrane's household experienced working-class poverty following the death of his father and grandfather, the Davis household was upper middle class, replete with servants and stylish clothes. And Dr. Miles Davis II was particularly indulgent of his namesake and favorite son. Miles was protected by his father, who spared no money in securing for his son the things he needed and wanted. Perhaps this difference played a role in the dissimilar styles of black manhood exhibited by Trane and Miles. Coltrane's leadership style and personal manner were gentle and compassionate. As a bandleader, he was capable of making decisions and changes and was always willing to lead the way. But he was also a nurturing spirit and never quite traded in his country, down-home ways for the urbane style that many jazz musicians sought and that Davis personified.

It is important to note that Miles, for all of his notorious profaneness, brashness, misogyny, and just plain cold-bloodedness, was also capable of the kind of generosity that has endeared him to band mates. The man who could be cool and confident, and who could play with the openness and vulnerability that Miles did, was a complex, bold, and pioneering version of midcentury masculinity.

Coltrane's courage and the strength exhibited in his virtuosity and intelligence were just as important an image for blacks, who were often portrayed as lacking in all of these qualities. But along with Trane's strength came gentleness, and with his brilliance came humility. His love for his people was guided by his love for God. Ultimately, however, it was the music each played that made them both important. And the music they played together was especially fine and crucial to the legacy that each man left behind.

By all accounts, John Coltrane was a gentle, soft-spoken man of few words; Miles Davis, though equally reserved, could be caustic, biting, and harsh. However, these qualities are reversed in their playing. When the two men came together in the mid-fifties, Coltrane's style already displayed a ferocity not evident in his personality, whereas Miles possessed an extraordinarily tender, lyrical approach to his instrument. Consequently, their methods of playing with their rhythm section were almost diametrically opposed. Trane was more verbose, with an extroverted style that belied his reputation for reticence and shyness. Davis was more economical, playing far fewer notes, thereby outlining a sketch of his message more so than rendering it explicitly. When the two began playing together in 1955, Davis was the clear leader. With a few gestures he set the tone of the music and controlled the band as deftly as Duke Ellington or Count Basie.

Given the stature both men came to hold in the jazz world as two giants—the gates through which subsequent players must come to the music—one might imagine their collaboration as one of competitive, if productive, combat: two musical geniuses battling it out night after night. According to all who knew and observed them, this was not the case. For one thing, Trane was too humble, and Miles, quite simply, was too cool. So the image of two masculine figures duking it out on the bandstand does not even approach the relationship between these two musical powerhouses. Miles and Trane were not like Picasso and Matisse, highly competitive friends whose competition spurred each to greater achievement. Like Ralph Ellison and Albert Murray, Miles and Trane were of the same generation, but Miles matured as an artist much earlier than did Trane. Their relationship would be one where Trane could stretch and grow artistically. Later, Coltrane would list Miles Davis as one of the two master teachers from whom he learned while playing in their bands (Thelonious Monk was the other). The relationship between Miles and Trane was not one fueled by competition, nor did one musician live enviously in the shadow of the other. Instead, their collaboration was more like an apprenticeship, with Miles as the master artist and Trane as the young, talented, questing acolyte. Drummer Rashied Ali, who saw the two play together on a number of occasions, recalled: "Miles was really the boss, I mean, of that band. Even though John played a lot longer . . . than Miles sometimes . . . Miles, I think he was like really the leader."

From Miles, Trane learned important lessons about pacing and how to sculpt memorable solos. Equally important, however, are the lessons that he gained about management, about putting a band together, and about the importance of establishing a unique band sound. An ardent student of music with uncanny discipline and diligence, Coltrane would not remain in Miles's shadow for long and in many ways would eclipse the trumpeter's importance in the music.

There is a photograph of the two of them, taken in a recording studio, that speaks volumes about them. Miles stands behind a hanging microphone, muted horn pointing down into the mike.

Miles Davis and John Coltrane during the *Kind of Blue* recording session, 1959.

He is in a characteristic Miles stance, graceful, poised, weight on right leg, left hip slightly tilted. Dark glasses—keeping us out—white shirt stark against his dark skin, long sleeves opened at the cuffs but almost echoing the bell of the horn. The shirt is tucked neatly into his pants. He is tight and fit, in full control, in top form. Miles *is* an aesthetic statement.

Behind him stands Trane. The most obvious thing about him is the horn positioned horizontally across his waist. He stands solidly on both feet, flat, grounded on the floor; there is no dancer's grace, but a determination that anchors him there. He is wearing an untucked, short-sleeved plaid shirt that fits tightly across a slight beer belly. Even the sleeves are a little tight. He is listening intently to what Miles is playing, hearing his way through his own response. Miles is the sure one, the center of attention, and the focus. For Miles, the music is the central component of a larger aesthetic project that includes fashion, painting, boxing, and self-creation. Trane, even when not playing, seems too focused on the music to be concerned about much else.

In a May 30, 1959, review of the New Miles Davis Quintet in *Down Beat,* the reviewer (possibly Nat Hentoff) wrote:

> *Miles is in wonderfully cohesive form here, blowing with characteristically personal, eggshell tone, muted on the standards, open on the originals and he continues to grow in his searching quality of being able to go so inside a song that he makes it fit him as if to order without injuring the essence of the work as first written. Coltrane, as Ira Gitler notes accurately, "is a mixture of Dexter Gordon, Sonny Rollins and Sonny Stitt." But so far there is very little Coltrane.*

Miles makes the song fit him in much the same way his tailor alters his clothing to his body. For this reviewer, Trane was working his way through the masters, searching, seeking his own voice. By the end of his tenure with Miles just two years later, no one would ever say there was very little Coltrane in his sound. By then, he had become the standard-bearer for all who would follow him on tenor.

Once it was time for Trane to move on, he did so with Miles's blessing and his gift of a soprano saxophone. Their relationship had always been conducted primarily on the bandstand and in the studio; there is little evidence of their interaction beyond that arena, so we must listen for their conversations in the music they made. Ali and saxophonist Sonny Fortune are two accomplished musicians in their own right who knew and worked with Trane and Miles, respectively. (The two now often perform mesmerizing duets together, a project they have maintained for two decades.) A conversation between Fortune and Ali best articulates the nature of communication between Miles and Trane:

> FORTUNE: *My working with Miles would suggest that {their communication} wasn't extensive. Miles wasn't a talker and Trane wasn't a talker. So you got to guess there's no talking.*
>
> ALI: *Not with words, anyway.*[7]

Not with words, anyway. It's in the music. Let's listen:

IT IS March 22, 1960, and the Miles Davis Quintet is playing at the Stockholm Concert Hall in Sweden. It is the last tour in which John Coltrane will play as a permanent member of Davis's band. On the set that night was a collection of blues and rhythm changes, standard fare for a jazz combo at the time, but also a new piece that would play a role in heralding another era in jazz composition and performance: "So What." Perhaps Miles Davis's most famous composition, it flows and floats through time in an evocative way, in part because of its modal character. One of a handful of musicians whose silences are always just as important as his played notes, Davis built the composition with a minimum of musical materials—a bass riff, a two-note motif for the horns played over a harmonic framework that itself includes only two chords.

On this occasion, we hear two master musicians giving statements that stand as testaments to the thoughts and feelings of the age—testaments as eloquent as any made in that era of American history, rife with both struggle and optimism. Full of passion and intelligence, simultaneously abounding in both power and subtlety, their performances represent the apotheosis of the Davis/Coltrane collaboration. We have a snapshot of what could happen when the "world's greatest band" coalesced enough to give voice to the lessons learned by each member over the years of the band's life. Coltrane had learned from Miles how to pace himself in a solo. Coltrane was always an original and able improviser with a nonpareil technique, a man whose horn spoke to the fundamental passions while simultaneously addressing the most complex thoughts of those striving for higher consciousness. On the songs recorded on the album released of this concert (and others from this tour currently available as bootleg recordings), one can hear some of the things that Trane learned from listening and playing with one of his two master teachers. Miles's influence is evident in the ways that Coltrane begins his improvisations with relatively concise formulations and reformulates the ideas again and again, gradually teasing out their implications and possibilities. Unlike the Coltrane who had joined the Miles Davis Quintet five years earlier, here Trane has learned to think in larger units, to develop his ideas over entire choruses rather than from chord to chord or from bar to bar. Following his own proclivities, through logical and thorough investigation and development, Coltrane stretches his ideas further during each chorus until it is finally clear that he is pointing toward the future of music and not simply reveling in his mastery of the existing forms. The rhythmic language that Coltrane uses is quite advanced, in that he found a way to swing without relying upon the time-honored string of eighth notes. It sounds jarringly as though he has allowed the full expression of his emotions to surface, not the controlled hip voice, but rather the rough-and-ready voice in which he can express anger, fear, and outrage as well as the more sublime emotions. Similarly, his range, in terms of how high he plays, at points exceeds the normal practice of the day, as does the level of adventurousness between the melodic lines and the harmonic underpinning of his improvisations. No longer does he restrict himself to playing within the bar lines, or limit himself to four- and eight-bar phrases that represented the jazz orthodoxy. Yet Coltrane has not abandoned the blues or the standard song forms from which these conventions arose; he extends their meaning through a sustained investigation of how far he can stretch them in this context.

If he were not moored by the rhythm section, which keeps swinging no matter what bombs he might lob into the mix, Coltrane just might have flown off into completely uncharted territory. As it is, he is clearly knocking at the door of an increased sense of freedom from the melodic and rhythmic conventions of bebop. Miles had given Trane free rein to develop and play as he saw fit. And on this tour, Coltrane played with an abandon and exploratory feeling greater than on any of his recordings to date. It was as if the Muses were announcing to him that he was now ready to make his own way, that he had arrived.

Part of the piquancy of listening to Coltrane at this point in time is the tension that he creates by pulling and stretching the music along new melodic contours and rhythmic configurations, while the context for his improvisations, the accompaniment by the rhythm section of Jimmy Cobb (drums), Wynton Kelly (piano), and Paul Chambers (bass), remains steadily in the mainstream tradition of hard swinging. The contrast between the funkiness of the steady beat and swing that Miles got out of his rhythm section and the almost furious exploration that Trane brought gave the band a powerful yet delicate balance. This band provided the kind of music you could pat your feet to, music signifying hipness. Someone seeking to impress and express urbanity and sexiness might bring a date to hear the Miles Davis group. At the same time, with Coltrane's contributions, this is also startlingly serious music. His sounds are more likely to induce trancelike attention than finger snapping or head bopping.

Although with hindsight we know that Coltrane was on the

verge of becoming one of the great bandleaders in the history of the music, on this outing it is Miles Davis who is the leader, and it is he who sets the tone of the music and provides Trane with the berth adequate to launch his musical flights. Davis's conception is one that takes the bird's-eye view; Miles is able to unfold his solo as an organic whole. (Jazz musicians refer to their aesthetic ideas and artistic praxis as their "conception.") With solos like this one, the listener understands the "tell a story" metaphor made famous by Lester Young and held dear by subsequent generations of improvisers. Each chorus builds logically upon the previous and without hurry or wasted motion provides a vast range of ideas and emotions shaped in all the registers of the horn. It is in the newly expanded range of Miles's trumpet playing that we can hear Coltrane's influence upon his bandleader. Coltrane's style included frequent trips to the altissimo register of the saxophone, officially above the classical range of the instrument. The altissimo register is the very high range of an instrument, akin to the falsetto range of the male voice. Like the falsetto voice, the altissimo usually carries an added tension and sometimes a certain coarseness to the sound. Often, Coltrane would punctuate his long, complicated melodies with sharp shrieks and cries at either extreme of the saxophone's range. With the low growls and honks of the bottom register and the screams of the upper register, Coltrane's horn combines the rawest sound ideals of the blues tradition right alongside the experimental harmonic and melodic treatments of modern music.

In the early part of Davis's career, when he was occasionally criticized for not following suit with the pyrotechnical displays expected of trumpet players after Dizzy Gillespie's bebop revelations, the older trumpeter explained to Miles that in order to play in the upper register, one had to hear in that register. Miles's increased ability to "hear" in the upper range of the trumpet was due no doubt not only to the exclamations that Coltrane used so meaningfully, but also to the fast, glissandolike scalar passages that he borrowed from Trane while en route to his target pitches. Coltrane sometimes played passages that contained very large intervals, intervals that are not amenable to singing and are therefore a bit removed from the smoothness for which many improvisers strive. Often starting in one register and ending in another, these lines brought the melodic range in excess of one octave in a way that gave hints of the disjointed leaps of which Coltrane had become so fond. It was as if a contralto voice had developed the range of a coloratura soprano. By extending the tonal range of his horn and his melodies, Miles used Coltranesque flourishes as more than ornamental appendages, but as an integral part of his overall aesthetic statement. By allowing for inclusion of the upper and lower ranges of the trumpet, he achieves more than virtuosity. Other trumpeters, such as Clifford Brown and Thad Jones, for instance, were more overtly virtuosic, but Miles added a mysterious personal quality by never allowing the display of his virtuosity to take precedence.

In his reserve, Davis is the opposite of Coltrane. He was poised in his playing and always seemed to know exactly what he wanted. Coltrane, by contrast, always seemed to be searching. He would try out ideas in rapid succession. Significantly,

Miles took the risk of allowing Trane to experiment both in public performances and on recordings; in so doing, Miles risked losing the support of critics as well as fans.

In part because of the differences between their instruments, the trumpet and the saxophone, and in part because of their different approaches to improvisation, Coltrane's and Davis's styles provided maximum contrast. These traits are full-blown in this example from the band's last tour with Wynton Kelly and Jimmy Cobb on piano and drums, respectively, but traces of what would be were present in the original Miles Davis Quintet with Red Garland and Philly Joe Jones, as can be heard in an example of one of the band's first recordings, "Round Midnight."

That band was a model of how to structure music *and* musical aggregations. It possessed the drama that Miles was raised on as a young bebopper standing next to Charlie "Bird" Parker on the bandstand. But Miles built his band around his melodic conception, which was one of the clearest and most beautiful of all time. Having Trane in the second horn chair gave Miles's front line the kind of balance between minimalist and pyrotechnical voices that Bird's band had earlier with a teenage Davis in the second horn chair. In the earlier band that had paired Dizzy and Bird, the front line featured two virtuosos whose brilliance was always in evidence. Their rendition of "Leap Frog," for instance, was built upon a friendly game of one-upmanship in that each plays a lot of ultrahip ideas on the changes, making incredibly fast, intricate melodies that fit together seamlessly. The front line of Bird and Miles was different. Rather than two virtuosos battling it out, urging each other on to more fantastic technical feats, Parker and Davis complemented each other and provided contrast. Beyond that, each man brought out the latent qualities of the other: In this combination, Bird became even more melodic, and Miles became a true bebop trumpeter. Miles and Trane's front line was modeled more after the Bird/Miles lineup than the Bird/Diz combination.

In addition to the front line, Miles's rhythm section was to die for. The propulsion that Paul Chambers gave the band was phenomenal. His tone was clear and resonant, his note choices intelligent, and his swing powerful and steady. As a bassist, he could solo with the kind of phrasing, articulation, and *content* that horn players used. And if that were not amazing enough, he could pick up his bow and take care of business there as well. With Philly Joe Jones on drums and Red Garland on piano, the rhythm section became a swinging affair, steady but pliant at the same time. On medium and up-tempo tunes, Jones and Garland regularly played in unison, improvising syncopated accents that added to the fiery sound of the band. The kind of strongly rhythmic comping that Jones and Garland supplied (aided, no doubt, by Garland's ability to play in block chords) helped to give the quintet a bigger sound. ("Comping" is taken from "accompaniment" and refers to the way that a musician—usually, but not always, the pianist— rhythmically and harmonically improvises a supportive background for another musician's solo.) It was as if a big band were playing shout choruses behind the soloist. Even though the band followed the small combo format made popular by

Charles Parker's quintet, the Miles Davis band had a sound reminiscent of the big bands. This was achieved largely by the arrangements, but also by the interplay between Jones and Garland. In big bands, the rhythmic accents are normally set and even written into the arrangements, but Philly Joe and Red were able to create equally tight figures on the fly. The improvised nature of their rhythmic counterpoint ensured that none of the suppleness or flexibility of the small combo was sacrificed to achieve the big band features.

Davis's impact on contemporary music was due both to his vision as a bandleader and to his unique playing style, especially when the tempos were slow. He brought something new to the art of ballad playing. The warmth and uniqueness of his tone are downright haunting. He has an uncanny mastery of time and form. Using only a few notes, exquisitely placed and phrased, he could imply larger ideas. Even when playing ballads, though, this band maintained its rawness. The *feeling* of going all out combined with superbly arranged presentations made the band seem a perfect emblem of the power and urgency of late 1950s black consciousness. Like the everyday people who valiantly waged the civil rights struggle, the music was dignified and well presented even though it held the hint of rage and turmoil underneath. Miles and Trane were steeped in black, southern traditions, musically and otherwise. As young professionals, both men sharpened their skills in the environs of New York bebop with all of its urbane sophistication. The Miles Davis sound came to maturity in this band; it was controlled and artful, but still hot.

That Miles and Trane were both great musical thinkers is made evident first, of course, by their skillful improvisations. While their approaches to improvisation in some ways were almost polar opposites, both were outstanding and original as soloists. In fact, each man's sound is recognizable after only one or two notes by any listener familiar with the music. The depth and breadth of their thinking, however, lay not only in the reflexes and instincts honed to perfection through discipline and talent, but also in important innovations in their compositions, arrangements, and conceptual approaches to music and to life.

This intelligence, combined with a passionate delivery and immense power, was something that Coltrane brought to the table when he joined the Miles Davis Quintet. But Coltrane's talent as a musician blossomed during his stint with Davis. In the wry words of multi-instrumentalist Howard Johnson (who would later work with Miles through his long association with Gil Evans), Miles's band was supposed to fail. In the eyes of his detractors, instead of building his band with the accepted leading players like saxophone colossus Sonny Rollins, "Miles had a junkie drummer, a cocktail pianist, a teenage bassist, and an out-of-tune saxophonist. Yet he sold a whole lot of records and made all the musicians eager to hear each one as it came out."[8]

According to Wallace Roney, Miles's protégé and apparently the only major trumpeter to be taken under his wing, Miles thought of this band as the greatest in the world not simply because of his alchemy, but also because of the individual talents of the band members. He saw Paul Chambers as the heir to his favorite bassists, Oscar Pettiford and Charles Mingus.

He especially admired Chambers's virtuosity. Miles loved Bud Powell and Thelonious Monk as the music's premier pianists. But Red was like Bud Powell with Nat "King" Cole's touch, just as Miles himself could be seen as Fats Navarro with Freddie Webster's tone. Like Miles, Red loved boxing. Garland was a professional and had even fought Sugar Ray Robinson. That he lost to a man that many consider the greatest boxer, pound for pound, was no dishonor. Garland had also played with Bird and played on his *Live at St. Nick's* album with Roy Haynes in 1950. Roney said that Miles thought Red was "hip and could play fast with that elegant thing."

The Chief was able to bring out each of these musicians' unique voice in such a way as to make hard swinging music that also seemed to promise something new. He excelled at bringing together the elements of personalities, talents, and musical concepts to create a band that was familiar and accessible while at the same time forceful and visionary. By adding to the tradition, or rather finding their unique voices within it, they were able to widen the scope of the music's articulations for future players.

Trane's and Miles's abilities to speak to new generations have made them resonate within our culture as more than just great or even innovative musicians. Trane's relentless development as a musician was astounding, and his courage was singular. He represented the triumph of black genius through discipline and integrity. His horn playing seemed visionary while he spoke to the spirits, and his humility made it seem possible for others to aspire to such. Poet, essayist, playwright, and jazz critic Amiri Baraka says of him, "Coltrane was the most humble person I ever met. You know, a person who is *truly* great with such humility."[9] Trane's music simultaneously made calls for radical change and for acknowledging the beauty and gravity of God's creation. It was complex and eventful enough to provide musical sustenance for a generation that was experiencing a concurrence of political struggle, cultural flowering, and social reconstruction. It captured a moment when the fate of black people was absolutely central to the future of the modern world.

There are times when two people come together for a moment to produce something extraordinary, a gift, so to speak, for the rest of us: an organization that aids the disenfranchised, a business, a piece of art, or—as is the case with Miles Davis and John Coltrane—a body of work. If the relationship is one in which each participant is pushed to his best while helping to create an atmosphere where the other shines as well, then the results often appear magical, and the collaboration seems to accomplish something that moves us all, listeners and players, to the next level. Such was the moment when these two gifted men came together in the mid-1950s. Both were formed by and helped to inform the burgeoning civil rights movement of the late 1950s and early 1960s. And both emerged as global icons for generations to follow.

LIKE ALL other biographers to date, we have no access to the conversations that took place between them. There is no known recorded dialogue between the two. In the beginning, when

Coltrane felt keenly his need to bring up his game and meet the expectations that attended being in such select company, he would ply the master with questions about music and about his methods and choices. This inquisitiveness was something that Miles admired in Trane's musical statements, but he found the fact that "Trane was always asking those mother-fucking questions" a turnoff. But Miles admired his serious-ness and the fact that he was always practicing. There was some musical instruction, but it turned out to be a two-way lesson conducted primarily in the medium of music. After a while, Miles would write things specifically for Trane, espe-cially during his second tenure with the band. Roney tells us that Miles believed that "Trane was a genius." He would write little things for Trane, who "would turn it upside down and play it five or six different ways." When Miles heard what his saxophonist had done with his ideas, he would be inspired to go even further. But Miles spoke to his band primarily through his horn. Roney attests to the various ways that Miles could signal to his band what he wanted by the way he phrased his ideas. Also, when it came to arranging, Miles could, with just a few changes and decisions, alter the character of a song. He could direct any other aspect of the music, but he did not in-terfere with how a musician soloed. By the time Coltrane was himself a master bandleader, he would rebuff his sidemen for asking what they should do: "I can just about play my horn; I can't tell you how to find your own way." As leaders, both men certainly set the musical direction of their groups, but they also valued band mates who could find their own voice and contribute originality as well as technical mastery.

Most of those who knew or worked with them cannot recall much of their verbal interaction. It is as though they led parallel lives, in the same time—indeed, next to each other—but crossed only in the music, on the bandstand, in the studio.

This book will focus on the historical and political times they shared and, more important, on the music they made. Yes, there will be personal details, but the music sits center. Hopefully by the end, we will have helped you to really listen, to hear their statements, conversations, and innovations. In seeking to understand the music they made, by joining them in their pursuits, we learn more about art, history, this music we call jazz, and human possibility as well.

PASS IT ON

Nobody starving in my home; nobody crying in my home, and if I got a home, you got one too! Grab it. Grab this land! Take it, hold it, my brothers, make it, my brothers, shake it, turn it, twist it, beat it, kick it, kiss it, whip it, stomp it, dig it, plow it, seed it, reap it, rent it, buy it, sell it, own it, multiply it and pass it on—can you hear me? Pass it on!

— TONI MORRISON, *Song of Solomon*

ONE IS OFTEN CALLED the Prince of Darkness, the other a saint, ever questing for the light. Both loom large upon the cultural landscape and seem to transcend their identities as musicians or entertainers. It is easy to think of them as individuals who sprang Topsy-like out of nowhere, without history, unattached to the generations that preceded them. If we do think of them in relation to previous generations, it is in the context of the musical tradition they help to challenge, develop, and redefine. We forget that they emerged from specific histories, families, and contexts that shaped the man each would become. And while each story tells us a great deal about these two musical geniuses, it also tells us about a period in the history of a nation that would lay the groundwork for the artist's quest for freedom in his music and, indeed, in his life.

Both Davis and Coltrane were born during an era known

variously as the Jazz Age, the Roaring Twenties, and the Harlem or New Negro Renaissance. The era has come to be defined by artists and intellectuals such as Langston Hughes, F. Scott Fitzgerald, W. E. B. Du Bois, Jelly Roll Morton, Duke Ellington, Bessie Smith, and Louis Armstrong. However, it is quite possible that none of these figures influenced the world into which Trane and Miles were born as much as Booker T. Washington or that first generation of black political figures and businessmen who emerged from the Reconstruction South, a time when the national government lent its might to help ensure the freedmen's and -women's passage into full citizenship.

When President Rutherford B. Hayes removed the last United States troops from the South in 1877, Reconstruction's fourteen-year experiment in multiracial democracy ended abruptly. Legal and extralegal means were applied to slow the progress of socially mobile African Americans and to submerge the vast majority into a vicious debt peonage system. The world into which Coltrane and Davis were born and the sensibilities that nurtured them were less those of the urban modernist movements than that of the post-Reconstruction South.

The title and epigraph of this section, "Pass It On," is taken from Toni Morrison's exquisite novel *Song of Solomon,* a meditation on black masculinity in twentieth-century North America, which investigates the roles that class and geography can play in personality development and political consciousness. The protagonist, Macon "Milkman" Dead III, is a self-centered, middle-class young man who acquires a sense of himself by learning about his family's history, especially the story of his great-grandfather Macon Dead I, a former slave and "the clever irrigator, the peach-tree grower, the hog slaughterer, the wild turkey roaster," who sixteen years out of slavery had "one of the best farms in Montour County." Like Macon Dead I, both Miles Davis's and John Coltrane's grandfathers were black men who had lived to see the promises of Reconstruction fade but struggled against all odds to live self-sufficient lives and provide opportunities and property for their heirs. And, like Macon Dead, these men would bequeath their male progeny a legacy and a sense of self-confidence as black men in a land and during a time when confident black men were deemed among the greatest threats to the racial and class status quo.

The first postslavery generation sought to rebuild and maintain families, educate their children, and acquire property. Most important, because they lived so close to the experience of slavery, they valued their hard-won freedom and sought safeguards for maintaining it even as the federal government, time and again, failed to guarantee their rights and safety and as southern states tried to return them to the status of chattel. They married and raised children who no longer could be owned by others. They built churches, fraternal and civil rights organizations, and schools. They also created unique cultural forms of entertainment like the blues and jazz. And a fortunate few acquired land.

Holding on to it would prove to be another struggle. There was no time or place where the antipathy toward blacks was stronger than when and where they were prosperous. In 1892,

Ida B. Wells, a journalist in Memphis, Tennessee, first studied the correlation between African American economic success and subsequent trumped-up charges that led to lynchings. With black codes enacted to peel back the social gains of the Reconstruction era and de facto sanctioning of lynch law, blacks were exposed to lethal violence for "offenses." Such offenses might include the failure to perform ritualized deference to whites in social settings (answering to demeaning names, stepping off the sidewalk to allow whites to pass, and so on) as well as owning well-appointed property, especially businesses and prosperous farms. In spite of threats by white supremacists and the theft of the Davis family's land, both Davis's and Coltrane's families were among those who established themselves as property-owning pillars of their communities, devoted to the steady climb up from slavery.

Three generations of black men have shared the name Miles Davis (herein referred to as Davis I, Dr. Davis, and Miles). Davis I seems to have been born in Georgia, approximately five years after the end of the Civil War. He inherited the spirit of those who struggled, fought for, and acquired their freedom, only to devote themselves to keeping it. In a spirit similar to that of the Exodusters, those freedmen and -women who left the lower South for the homesteading lands of Kansas in 1879, Davis I migrated from northwest Georgia to Arkansas. Although the Exodusters preceded him by a generation, what historian Nell Painter writes of them rings true for Davis I as well: They "were interested in land, schools and protecting their lives and their Civil Rights."

In Arkansas, Davis I was both an accountant and a farmer who owned land in Nobel Lake. Listed in both the 1900 and the 1910 censuses as head of the household, he fathered a total of ten children with his first and second wives. His second wife, Ivey, was the woman Miles knew as his grandmother. Miles would later cherish memories of visiting his grandfather's farm and credit those trips south with having first introduced him to the music of the rural black church. In a now famous quotation, the musician recalled:

> *I also remember how the music used to sound down there in Arkansas, when I was visiting my grandfather, especially at the Saturday night church. Man, that shit was a motherfucker. I guess I was about six or seven. We'd be walking on these dark country roads at night and all of a sudden this music would seem to come out of nowhere, out of them spooky-looking trees that everybody said ghosts lived in. I remember somebody would be playing a guitar the way B. B. King plays. And I remember a man and a woman singing and talking about getting down! Shit, that music was something, especially that woman singing. But I think that kind of stuff stayed with me, you know what I mean? That kind of sound in music, that blues, church, back-road funk kind of thing, that southern, midwestern, rural sound and rhythm. I think it started getting into my blood on them spook-filled Arkansas back-roads after dark when the owls came out hooting. So when I started taking music lessons I might have already had some idea of what I wanted my music to sound like.[1]*

This was the landscape that held the history of slavery and Reconstruction, that helped to shape the development of the blues, and it is this southern, deeply rooted black sound that echoed in Miles's playing throughout his career.

Davis I provided access to this world and served as the link between the generations that came before and those that would follow. He also instilled the values of economic self-sufficiency and the primacy of education in his children as they would in their children. Two of his sons, Miles Davis II and Ferdinand, became an oral surgeon and Harvard graduate, respectively. After his graduation, Ferdinand Davis went on to become editor of *Color* magazine—an African American magazine that began publication in 1944, one year before *Ebony*. Other siblings (there were nine Davis children: six sons and three daughters) became teachers, politicians, and civil rights leaders in their own communities. As was the case with thousands of blacks who migrated—first west to Kansas and Oklahoma and later north and west to the mid-Atlantic states and Illinois, Michigan, and California—each generation of the Davis family also migrated in search of opportunity and freedom from the limitations placed on them by racism.

In 1900, the year of Dr. Davis's birth, black Arkansans had been disenfranchised and denied access to public facilities by Jim Crow laws. However, as was the case elsewhere, this racially hostile environment saw black communities create a culture of opposition and resistance as well as build their own institutions. A strong black nationalist bent, encouraged by their exclusion, found them developing an independent black business community in the early 1900s. According to historian LeRoy T. Williams, by 1902 John E. Bush founded the

Colored Men's Business League, and in 1903 black banks were opened in Pine Bluff and Little Rock. The state boasted a number of black newspapers, hotels, restaurants, beauty salons, and other service-oriented businesses. These business achievements undergirded efforts to build and sustain institutions that educated black children. It wasn't only the cities that witnessed efforts at black self-determination. In 1919, Robert L. Hill, a black sharecropper from Phillips County, organized the Progressive Farmers and Household Union, "a self-help group based on the principles of Booker T. Washington's Negro Business League."[2] In the early decades of the twentieth century, lawyer Scipio A. Jones founded the Black and Tan political ticket. In 1920, they actually ran a candidate for governor, John A. Blount. The Arkansas into which Dr. Davis was born was "a region characterized by a rich history of Afro-American struggle and accomplishment," militant activism by sharecroppers and urban dwellers with a "tradition of self-help and political mobilization."[3]

As might be expected, black Arkansans' efforts to establish a self-sufficient community met with great resistance from whites. In 1900, there were four documented lynchings in the state, three of them black men. By the time Dr. Davis was twenty years old, over eighty more suffered the same fate, among them a number of black women. In October 1919, police officers opened gunfire on a meeting of the Progressive Farmers and Household Union. The ensuing events led to the Elaine riot at Hoops Spur in Phillips County, Arkansas, which left five whites and almost two hundred blacks killed in a period of five days. More than one thousand blacks were arrested, and sixty-seven were tried and convicted for murder and insurrection. Black sharecroppers and tenant farmers would not attempt to organize again until fifteen years later, when they founded the Southern Tenant Farmers' Union.

Davis I didn't escape this wave of violence and dispossession. He avoided a violent death, but in 1961, Dr. Davis told an interviewer from *Ebony* magazine: "[My father] was driven from his extensive holdings." Miles Davis biographer Jack Chambers has written that "Davis's grandfather was removed from his land, probably because his holdings outstripped too conspicuously those of his white neighbors or perhaps because his bookkeeping jobs made him too knowledgeable about the business dealings of the whites. For whatever reason Miles Davis's grandfather lived much of his adult life under the threat of violence from white men."[4] Despite that, he passed on his entrepreneurial sensibility to his children. Among the many things Miles inherited from his father and his paternal grandfather were business acumen, a sense of racial pride, confidence—arrogance, even—an awareness of the constant threat of racial violence, and with it a lifelong distrust of white men.

Miles's father, Dr. Davis, attended Arkansas Baptist College (ABC), Lincoln University, and Northwestern University's School of Dentistry. At ABC he met and married Cleota Henry, a beautiful and elegant young woman who had been born and raised in North Little Rock, Arkansas. The couple set up house in Alton, Illinois, where their first child, Dorothy

Mae, was born in 1924. Two years later, Cleota gave birth to Miles.

When Miles was three, the young family moved to East St. Louis. At the time, East St. Louis was one of America's poorest cities. It had been the site of horrific race riots from May to July 1917.[5] Twelve years later, when the Davis clan relocated, the city was deeply impoverished and still bore the stains of these earlier events. By the time the Davises' third child, Vernon, was born, the Depression had arrived and Dr. Davis found himself losing business; often he was paid in food instead of dollars. Nonetheless, the family managed to survive and maintain an upper-middle-class status: They dressed well, employed maids and cooks, and attended the city's prestigious black church, St. Paul's Baptist Church, throughout the 1930s.

Dr. Davis's economic fortunes improved when the country entered World War II and East St. Louis became a site of wartime industry. Eventually, he bought two hundred acres of land, where he raised horses and prize hogs. The younger Miles became an adept horseman and often returned to his father's farm throughout his life, especially when he needed the mental grounding and healing provided by home.

Both Dr. Davis and Miles note that they came from a long line of musicians, many of whom were slaves trained to play at their masters' social functions. According to Miles, most of his musical ancestors were fiddlers, as were many enslaved musicians. Significantly, a number of ads for runaway slaves note them to have been fiddlers as well. So it is quite possible that both the affinity for music and the love of freedom are well represented in the Davis family tree.

Despite this family history, Dr. Davis was discouraged from pursuing a musical career (probably as a pianist or violinist) and chose instead to seek professional training as a dentist and oral surgeon. Years later, Dr. Davis recalled, "My father . . . was born six years after the Emancipation and forbade me to play music because the only place a Negro could play then was in barrel-houses."[6] Although Dr. Davis was dissuaded from playing music, his wife played piano, though not frequently. Years later, her son Miles recalled discovering his mother playing the piano and expressing his surprise at her musical ability.[7] Miles also recalled his mother "sang like Roberta Flack." And his grandmother taught organ. While Miles's autobiographical musings focus a great deal on his musical "fathers," the uncles, godfathers, teachers, and other musicians who ushered him into the world of music, the women in his family were musically significant as well. After all, it was the sound of the woman's voice from that Arkansas night that would haunt his playing for the rest of his life.

By the time he turned thirteen, Miles had a typical black middle-class life. He delivered the *Chicago Defender,* perhaps the most important black paper of the early decades of the twentieth century. He played street games and followed boxing. Dr. Davis doted on his namesake, lavishing him with gifts and encouraging his aspirations. Whenever the boy demonstrated an interest in something, his father would buy the necessary equipment and pay for the lessons. Because he was small and dark-skinned, he was often teased and taunted. Dr. Davis bought him boxing gloves and saw to it that he learned to defend himself. (Miles would maintain a lifelong interest in boxing, even entering the ring himself.) When young Davis got into fights for wearing short pants, his grandfather suggested he ask his father for knickers. Dr. Davis bought him a striped suit with knickers. He continued to buy his son fashionable clothing throughout his teen years. Well-dressed children were a source of great pride to African Americans, not only because they were a demonstration of their parents' prosperity, but also because personal style and grooming made a public statement about the "race." As we shall see, Miles continued to be fashion conscious throughout his life. In the last decade of his life while schooling his only protégé, Wallace Roney, Miles would model various outfits for him, declaring, "I can't play unless I look good."[8]

According to Miles, his father never hit him. However, he did recall his mother hitting him. Although Mrs. Davis appears to have been much less doting than her husband, both parents were supportive and protective. Miles's mother extricated him from gang fights. She seems to have been the family disciplinarian and standard-bearer. When he decided he wanted to go to New York instead of Fisk University, mother and son began to argue. He cursed at her; she slapped him. She called his father and said, "Your son is crazy." To which his father replied, "Remember that the next time and leave him alone." It is not insignificant that Dr. Davis failed to chastise his son for cursing at his mother.

The boy learned complicated and disturbing lessons about relations between the sexes from his parents. At home, Miles's parents fought a great deal, often in front of the children. Miles recalled witnessing his father hitting his mother—a practice he unfortunately would adopt as an adult. The parents argued and cursed at each other constantly. Profanity was simply a way of life. Miles noted that the first thing his father said when he awoke each day was, "Shit." (According to their peers, all the Davis children were adept at cursing.) Eventually, Dr. and Mrs. Davis separated and then divorced when Miles was about fifteen years old, though they had already spent a lot of time apart before that.

Although their relationship continued to be a tense one, both parents were very devoted to their children and encouraged them in their pursuits. And both of them insisted upon a sense of racial pride. Mrs. Davis told her son, "Don't ever let me catch you Tomming for white folks." According to Miles, his father, like Malcolm X's father, was a Garveyite, a follower of the black nationalist leader, founder of the Back to Africa movement and organizer of the largest mass movement of blacks in the twentieth century. Miles's biographers have disputed this. However, even if Dr. Davis never joined Marcus Garvey's organization, the Universal Negro Improvement Association, he certainly was a greater adherent to racial separatism than to the more integrationist philosophies that would come to dominate black activism.

Both Dr. Davis and his wife were strong proponents of black pride and self-reliance. They viewed education, property ownership, and professional careers as protection from some of the strictures of American racism. Mrs. Davis had hoped her son would become a dentist like his father. She didn't believe musicians made any money. Even after he became a successful musician, she never seemed impressed with his choice of profession or his musical accomplishments. When she did concede to his interest in music, Mrs. Davis wanted her son to play violin, but from a very early age Miles expressed interest in the trumpet. When he was ten, a friend of his father's, Dr. John Eubanks, presented him with a cornet, and Dr. Eubanks's uncle, a professional musician, Horace Eubanks, gave him his first lessons. In sixth grade, he began to take weekly formal lessons with Elwood C. Buchanan, a local trumpet player who had toured with the famous Andy Kirk Orchestra and has been acknowledged as one of the architects of the St. Louis sound of trumpet playing. Eventually Davis took lessons with Joseph Gustat, who played trumpet with the St. Louis Symphony. For his thirteenth birthday, his father gave him his first trumpet. Thirteen is the age when many young men go through rites of passage that seek to usher them into manhood. Davis's rite included the gift of the horn, which would become for him, as for many others, a symbol of masculinity.

Even before he began to play in his school band, Miles performed at a dance in a trio that included Horace Eubanks. This is an indication of his talent, skill, and professionalism even at an early age. Before the proliferation of conservatory-style jazz programs, professional musicians did not necessarily come through the ranks of school educators, though there were many dedicated music educators who turned out impressive lists of accomplished students. By starting his music profession independent of school, Miles was demonstrating that he had the individual motivation and moxie that it took to become one of the cats. His musicianship gained him the respect of his peers, and his home became the gathering place for aspiring young musicians who eventually formed their own band. It was during this period that he began to develop his own style.

Miles especially liked the style of players who came through St. Louis from Oklahoma. There was an identifiable midwestern sound, which was more mellow than brassy. The sound never sacrificed tone for flashy technique, and the midwesterners gloried in their individual sounds more so than their mastery of the licks of their favorite players. Later, Miles claimed that not only he but also Clark Terry and all other musicians from St. Louis were more influenced by the Oklahoma sound than by that of New York. His adherence to some of the principles of music absorbed from those of the Oklahoma musicians marked his sound and approach as radically different from those of virtually all of the beboppers and their stylistic heirs. Unlike so many of his contemporaries, Dizzy Gillespie, who represented the epitome of bebop trumpet playing with his extended range, uncommon agility, and technical facility, was not a foundational model for Miles.

Initially, the young Davis was more drawn to the cornet, which is a smaller and mellower version of the trumpet. He valued the bigness and melodiousness of the sound as well as the slower pace with which it was played. Throughout most of his career on trumpet, Miles continued to re-create this beautiful sound, played mostly in the middle registers, and would refrain from technical flashiness. The importance of sound to the Oklahoma musicians was legendary—one need only think of the likes of a Jimmy Rushing, the blues shouter who gained fame with the Count Basie Orchestra. Rushing's fellow Oklahoman Ralph Ellison, who was a trumpeter and composer before he was an author, writes of one exercise that required holding a note for as long as he could. Practicing "long tones" is the tedious but necessary exercise for building a superior tone. These musical values did not come from an inferior knowledge of harmony and improvisational acumen. Miles would later express disappointment about what he found musically in New York. When he was in St. Louis, he had thought that everyone in New York was like Dizzy, but after visiting the city, he decided that the Oklahoma/St. Louis musicians "was the ones."

As a teenager Miles played ballrooms, not clubs, in St. Louis and attended jam sessions with professional musicians who arrived off the boats in Brooklyn, Illinois. His favorite trumpeters were Clark Terry and Harry James, two popular players of the time. Terry was often in St. Louis and eventually took the young Miles under his wing, sometimes taking him to jam sessions.

Under Buchanan's guidance, Miles began to develop his own sound while still influenced largely by musicians of the Midwest. He learned to play classical music as well as blues and country. In school, most of the young musicians could play loud, but Buchanan encouraged him to play within his range and to play with less vibrato. Davis couldn't play loud, but because of his knowledge of music (Eubanks had taught him the chromatic scale, and he brought that to music class), he could solo.

Sixteen-year-old Miles was so obsessed with music that he had little time for girls, but in 1942 he met Irene Cawthorn. Two years his senior, Irene was beautiful and hip but came from a poor family and lived in a bad neighborhood. Miles's family did not approve, but in spite of this, or perhaps because of it, the young couple was inseparable. It was Irene who challenged Miles to ask Eddie Randle for a job with his Blue Devils, a St. Louis dance band. Randle hired him. Once he began to play with Randle's band, Miles gained a great deal of exposure with the public but also with older musicians like Sonny Stitt and Illinois Jacquet, who took an interest in him and often visited him at home to give lessons. To Miles's amazement, he also had the opportunity to meet and speak with Charlie Parker, who encouraged him to come to New York.

Soon New York was all Miles could think about. He began to make plans to leave the Midwest for the city of his dreams. Although his mother wanted him to attend Fisk, Irene encouraged him to go to Juilliard. According to biographer John Szwed, it was Irene who wrote away for the applications.

Just as Miles finished high school in 1944, Irene became pregnant. Although he wanted to marry her, Dr. Davis wouldn't give the underage Miles the legal permission he needed. Instead he tried to discredit Irene and suggested that the child may have been fathered by someone else. Once again, he may have contributed to his son's lifelong distrust of women. He even offered to pay for an abortion. Miles refused, and though he did not marry Irene, the two lived together as husband and wife. When he moved to New York to attend Juilliard, she would join him.

In the spring of the same year, Billy Eckstine's band came to St. Louis, and Miles found his way to the Plantation Club, where he listened to their rehearsals, talked with the musicians, and begged to sit in with one of the hippest bands of the time. Dizzy Gillespie, Art Blakey, Charlie Parker, Gene Ammons, and Sarah Vaughan—they were the embodiment of the style and sound of the new music. On the night the band's trumpet player, Buddy Anderson, fell ill, Dizzy Gillespie asked Miles to replace him. It was both a dream come true and a nightmare. Although Miles knew all the parts by heart, he had trouble keeping up. But the bug had bitten him, and shortly thereafter he resolved to follow his idols to New York.

Miles was clearly talented, dedicated, and disciplined. He was also supported, encouraged, and nurtured by his family and members of his community—friends of the family, his teachers, older musicians, and even his girlfriend. His family's economic status provided certain protection and kept many of the harsher realities of segregation at bay. The combination all but assured his success. His musical training would give him a foot up when he went to New York in September 1944. Although he would always look up to Bird and Diz, many of the bebop icons were no more musically savvy than he. And he would take with him his unique sound, which would remain a trademark throughout his career. When Miles entered the

Miles Davis's embouchure was especially relaxed and free from the apparent strain displayed by many trumpeters. His sound, more beautiful and vulnerable than most, was a revelation.

company of the first-rate New York musicians, he did so with an already developed and individual style.

LIKE MILES, John Coltrane came of age in a close-knit but racially segregated community. While Davis's family history is filled with men named Miles, Coltrane's is dominated by a number of women named Alice. Less is known about his father's family. Because his father and maternal grandfather died before he entered his teens, he grew up under the stronger influence of his mother and her older sister. Even his sole de facto sibling, his cousin, Mary Alexander (for whom he would write and record "Cousin Mary"), was female. This might explain the difference in the personalities of the two musical giants. Trane, the gentler of the two, certainly had greater respect for the women in his life.

Coltrane's mother's family, the Blairs, was a prominent black family in High Point, North Carolina. His maternal grandparents, William Wilson Blair and Alice Virginia Leary, both were born in 1859. David Tegnell, a meticulous Coltrane scholar, asserts that although W. W. Blair and his wife had been born slaves, they were "freed by the Civil War." Until then, three generations of Blairs had been owned by Joseph Blount Skinner and his son Tristrim Lowther Skinner.[9]

Each grandparent could remember the Civil War and had come of age during Reconstruction and its aftermath. They witnessed the promises and disappointments of the era. Black North Carolinians met these challenges by organizing and creating a number of self-help and uplift organizations. Although North Carolina had fewer lynchings than many other southern states, it was no stranger to racial violence. In the 1890s, poor white farmers and blacks began to form alliances through the Populist and Republican parties. In 1892, the coalitions succeeded in taking votes from the Democrats, but the Democratic Party soon countered with a platform of racial politics. By 1898, the Democrats helped to spread a reign of racial terrorism that culminated in the Wilmington race riot.

When William and Alice Blair married in 1882, their home state was already growing hostile to the aspirations of its black citizens. A number migrated north, in search of greater freedom and opportunity. But those who stayed built political organizations and educational institutions that would lay the foundation for the future stages of the black freedom struggle. Coltrane's mother, Alice Gertrude Blair, the seventh of eight children, was born in 1898. Before her tenth birthday, the family had left North Carolina for Tampa, Florida.

Like Miles Davis, John Coltrane had a family history of landownership, self-sufficiency, and experience with racial terror. It is believed that William Blair, a prominent activist and preacher, had to leave North Carolina because of his activism. The youngest Blair child, John, recalled the Ku Klux Klan's threats against the family and surmised that shortly thereafter the family moved, leaving their land, which was eventually taken from them and sold. These stories were passed down to younger generations and helped to shape and form John's own identity.

By 1920, the family, all literate, returned to North Carolina, where Reverend Blair pastored the St. Stephen African Methodist Episcopal (AME) Zion Church in High Point. There, he also helped to build a school, later attended by his grandson.

In 1921, Alice enrolled in Livingstone College in Salisbury, North Carolina. Musically talented, she sang and played the piano. Syeeda Andrews, John Coltrane's stepdaughter (for whom he wrote "Syeeda's Song Flute"), recalled him telling her that the young Alice had a beautiful voice and wanted to sing opera and popular tunes but was prevented from doing so by her religious father. Instead she accompanied the church choir on piano. Her love of music would later help her to encourage her only child to pursue his own musical ambitions. When she graduated in May 1925, Alice moved to Hamlet, where she knew friends of her family, the Reverend William H. Coltrane of the AME Church and his family. In late 1925, Alice married the reverend's son, John Robert Coltrane. Both Alice, a seamstress, and John, a tailor, were skilled tradespeople, an exception in a time and place where many blacks continued to be tenant farmers and sharecroppers.

After a stillbirth, Alice gave birth to John William Coltrane in 1926. Within months, she and her husband moved to Alice's family home in High Point. Although William Blair spent months away from home visiting various churches, he continued to be a strong presence in the household. Years later, Coltrane told an interviewer:

> My grandfather—he was the dominant cat in the family. He was most well versed, active politically. He was more active than my father, {who} was a tailor; . . . {my father} never seemed to say much. He just went about his business, and that was it. But my grandfather, he was pretty militant, you know. Politically inclined and everything.

John Coltrane acquired his father's quiet sensibility, but his grandfather's influence would become apparent as well. Like his grandfather, the adult John Coltrane acquired a library of books about black history and literature; and like both his grandfathers, he would also become very spiritual. John lived with his parents, his maternal grandparents, his aunt, and his first cousin, Mary. During the summer, he and Mary often traveled with their grandfather to Wadesboro, a town in southern North Carolina where Grandfather Blair spent much of his time as a presiding elder of the AME Zion Church.

While the elder Coltrane was quiet and reserved, he did express himself through music, playing both the ukulele and the violin. Years later, his son recalled: "My family was passionate about music, and my father played the violin well." In addition to being exposed to music at home, he probably sang with other students under the guidance of Julia Hall at Leonard Street Elementary School.

In 1938, the family suffered a series of blows that would affect young John forever. Reverend Blair died on December 11, 1938, of pneumonia, and less than a month later, John R. Coltrane died of stomach cancer. On April 26, 1939, Coltrane's grandmother Alice died of breast cancer. Shortly thereafter, on the eve of his adolescence, John began to play alto horn and clarinet, quickly falling into what would be a lifelong habit of constant practice. Many who knew him saw music as his attempt to fill the void left by the devastating loss of his grandparents and his father. Like Miles, John became obsessed with music as he entered his teen years, but his obsession was accompanied by a profound sense of loss and melancholy. Syeeda says that she always heard a kind of sadness in his playing: "It was as if he were looking for something."[10]

In the fall, following the deaths, Coltrane enrolled in high school. Although he had been a superlative student in elementary school, his grades now began to falter. He became more and more distressed at the Jim Crow practices that demanded black students receive old books, worn athletic uniforms, and the like from white schools. As an adult, he would strongly dislike playing in the South. Syeeda recalls he never wanted her to visit there, either.

By the time he was thirteen, he began to take formal music lessons through a community band organized by Reverend Warren B. Steele. The band played marches, and a small group of them also met at John's house to play jazz. By 1940, with the help of the PTA, Reverend Steele and the members of the community band organized a high school band for William Penn High School. John was very disciplined, practiced incessantly, and took lessons with Grayce W. Yokley, who directed the band at William Penn. Eventually, inspired by his idol, Johnny Hodges (who played alto sax), John decided to focus on the saxophone.

The middle-class status that might have protected the Blair-Coltrane family from the harshest elements of segregation was lost with the deaths of Reverend Blair and Coltrane Sr. Now the household included two single women, Alice and her sister, Bettie, and their children, John and Mary. The two women found work at a local country club and took in boarders. Before John graduated high school, his mother and his aunt moved to Philadelphia in search of work. Following his graduation in the spring of 1943, John joined them. There he enjoyed greater mobility and freedom than he did in the South, but the pace of the urban streets and their inhabitants were unfamiliar to the young man. John found work first at a sugar refinery and then at the Campbell's Soup Company factory across the bridge in Camden, New Jersey. He shared an apartment in North Philadelphia with his aunt Bettie and cousin Mary. Mother Alice, who worked as a live-in domestic servant, joined them on the weekends. John continued to pursue his music, and the three women encouraged his efforts. His mother bought him a used alto saxophone, and their minister allowed him to practice in the church whenever he wanted. Eventually, his mother even urged him to devote himself to his music full-time. This type of encouragement would also be the case later on when his first wife, Naima, told him that he would never be fulfilled if he chose postal work instead. That these women encouraged and supported him at the expense of their own financial stability is not insignificant. Some black Americans believe that the difficult material circumstances of many black women have prevented them from supporting the artistic ambitions of black men. This certainly was not the case for John Coltrane.

In 1944, a year after his arrival in Philadelphia, Coltrane began to attend the Ornstein School of Music, where he took saxophone lessons and theory classes. There he met a number of other young aspiring musicians. It wasn't long before he began to acquire a reputation around the city. Rashied Ali was one of the admiring musicians who would later have a significant impact on Coltrane's career, when Ali would become the innovative drummer for Coltrane's last working band in the two years before Coltrane's untimely death. Ali recalls that as a boy, he and his friends would ride their bikes to Coltrane's home and sit outside the window in order to hear him practice. Trane had become a hero to some of the neighborhood youth.

Though they had not met each other yet, Davis and Coltrane seemed to be traveling along parallel lines: Two young men, recognized early in life for their musical talents and having the full support of their families and their communities, were embarking on musical careers. Both were products of a middle-class upbringing: Although Trane's family did not have the financial resources of the Davises, they shared similar aspirations and values. Both came from families who accomplished remarkable things in the face of tremendous obstacles—families who demonstrated great capability but also experienced disenfranchisement, bitterness, and the constant threat of racial violence. That their families were able to achieve and to protect their children from the harshest elements of racial segregation seems to have given each young man a sense of racial pride, a belief in the abilities of his people and himself. On the other hand, the difficulties their families faced gave each a sense of trepidation about the world that awaited him. This sense of racial confidence and belief in black possibility would allow Davis and Trane to recognize the genius of the music they loved and would push them to pursue their art with complete dedication and passion.

THE BIRTH OF A NEW FREEDOM

By 1954, it became evident to all that African Americans, like their
counterparts in the colonial world, would no longer wait for the birth of a
new freedom.

—ROBIN KELLEY AND EARL LEWIS, *To Make Our World Anew*

WHILE JACKIE ROBINSON WAS BREAKING BARRIERS on a baseball
field in Brooklyn, across the river in the nightclubs of Manhattan a generation of musicians was breaking barriers as well.
These young people, many of them recent migrants to the city,
were taking jazz in a new direction. The new music, named
bebop by the press, seemed to embody the sense of urgency
and unrest of the time. It was "modern music" to the musicians who created it. And like other modern arts, it was somewhat abstract and idiosyncratic. Bebop melodies, usually
played in unison by a saxophonist and a trumpeter, were complicated and serpentine, with sudden shifts and turns. The
rhythms were often as jagged as the leaps in the melodies, and
the tempos were lightning fast. The improvisations doubled
the already quick tempos of the rhythm section and were as
harmonically advanced as they were melodically intricate. An
expanded choice of notes is one of the features that made this
music sound more complex than earlier styles of jazz. Tones

that previously would have been considered dissonant and aesthetically inappropriate came to be viewed as relatively consonant and eventually even commonplace. To the uninitiated, these note choices could sound harsh and discordant, but to the cognoscenti, they were hip and provocative.

The music communicated the longings, postures, and desires for greater freedom of the emerging generation that had reached adulthood during the war years: freedom to explore one's political and aesthetic sensibilities without reprimand or violence, freedom to receive remuneration and recognition for one's labor, and freedom to pursue one's vision. That this era gave birth to bebop as well as hard-driving gospel and frantic rhythm and blues is not surprising.

Miles Davis and John Coltrane were part of this generation, and their early careers developed in this atmosphere of rapid cultural change. They had come of age musically when the United States entered the war against fascism. It was also a time when black Americans exposed the hypocrisy of a nation fighting against racial supremacists abroad while supporting Jim Crow laws at home. If the Germans waged war and genocide in the name of white supremacy, the United States continued to be a nation steeped in a similar ideology: The everyday lives of black people were testament to this sad fact. During World War I, many black leaders encouraged African Americans to put their demands for racial justice on the back burner. They argued that by demonstrating their patriotism, their willingness to die for their country, they would be deemed worthy of the rights of first-class citizenship. Race riots, lynching, continuing poverty, disenfranchisement, and lack of economic opportunity taught them otherwise. During World War II, Adam Clayton Powell and Bayard Rustin, along with publications like the *Chicago Defender,* insisted on the Double V: Victory at Home and Victory Abroad. Most black people, across lines of class and region, refused to remain silent on issues of racial discrimination and terrorism at home while they fought the war overseas.

By the beginning of World War II, thousands of ordinary blacks left the South to escape Jim Crow and to find work in the war industry. They fled to cities such as Los Angeles, Oakland, Chicago, Detroit, Philadelphia, and New York; each of these cities would become centers of black music. The years between 1940 (the U.S. entrance into World War II) and 1954 (*Brown v. Board of Education*) witnessed some of the greatest changes in U.S. race-based domestic policy since the Reconstruction era. In 1944, *Smith v. Allwright* destroyed white primaries in the South. Along with poll taxes and property and literacy tests, all-white primaries were yet another measure southern states had used to disenfranchise blacks. Unable to vote in primary elections, African Americans were barred from the nomination process, thereby preventing the election of candidates who might be sympathetic to their goals. In 1946, *Morgan v. Virginia* deemed segregated seating on interstate public transportation unconstitutional. By 1947, the first group of Freedom Riders, an interracial group of young Americans, black and white, traveled south to test compliance with the ruling. Many were beaten and jailed. In 1948, a number of important legislative and governmental actions would strike a blow against white supremacy: Restrictive covenants—placed on deeds to ensure that homes would be sold only to "specific" buyers or to ensure that neighborhoods remained white—were outlawed. The Democratic Party split in two, with former vice president Henry Wallace, a staunch advocate of black civil rights, forming the Progressive Party, while Strom Thurmond led a group of southern Democrats, the Dixiecrats, in an effort to preserve segregation. On July 26, 1948, President Truman issued Executive Order 9981, effectively desegregating the armed services.

Legally, these challenges to Jim Crow culminated in the *Brown v. Board of Education* decision, which overturned the infamous *Plessy v. Ferguson* ruling of 1896 and in so doing attempted to dismantle half a century of state-sanctioned apartheid. But the legal and political arenas were not the only places where struggles ensued. Accompanying battles were fought in the pages of newspapers and books, in concert halls, on the playing fields, and on the streets. In 1943, Harlem and Detroit erupted in racial violence around issues of housing and police brutality.

For Miles, this quest for collective political freedom paralleled his own quest to liberate himself from the racism that sought to limit his ambitions as a man and as an artist. At the same time, he hoped to free himself from the legacy of Bird and Dizzy.

When eighteen-year-old Davis first arrived in New York in 1944, he intended to attend the Juilliard School. However, he soon became immersed in the jazz scene that extended from Harlem to 52nd Street to Greenwich Village. Within weeks of his arrival, he hooked up with one of his idols and most important teachers, Dizzy Gillespie. Soon, "Diz" became an older brother figure and Miles was a frequent visitor in his household. While Gillespie's wife, Lorraine, threw out other visiting musicians who lingered too long, Miles was always welcome to remain. He would stay for hours, soaking up the knowledge and wisdom that the older trumpeter shared. Shortly after hooking up with Diz, Davis found Charlie Parker in a Harlem club called Heatwave. Before long, Davis and Parker were roommates, and Miles soon was sharing the bandstand with his idols, two of the most significant architects of bebop. Before year's end, Irene joined him in New York, leaving their daughter, Cheryl, in East St. Louis. The couple shared an apartment on 147th Street between Broadway and Riverside. Parker moved to an apartment upstairs.

Davis credited his time spent with Bird and Dizzy as attendance in the "University of Bebop." In the winter of 1944, he was already playing at the Spotlite on 52nd Street with Parker, Teddy Walters, Curly Russell, Al Haig, and Max Roach. For Miles, the music he heard on 52nd Street was his ultimate musical education. There, he first fell in love with the softness of Billie Holiday and Lester "Prez" Young.

As a teenager in East St. Louis, Miles imagined that everyone in New York played like Bird and Diz, but once in New York City, he learned that they stood out even in the heady environment of the Big Apple. In spite of his youth, he was quite advanced musically. This was the result of the high quality of preparation he had received in St. Louis. Amazingly, by the spring of 1945 he was playing on 52nd Street with Coleman Hawkins (nicknamed "Bean" because he was so smart), Budd Johnson, and other luminaries.

Throughout his life, Miles regarded the variety and quality of music available on "the street" as the highlight of his life. He did a stint with Earl Hines's orchestra, one of the greatest and most innovative big bands ever (despite its lack of financial success). Of course, Count Basie's band was the sound of Kansas City and immortalized as one of the most swinging bands in history. But in spite of Miles's pride in his midwestern musical heritage, "Earl Hines had the band, not Basie."

Hines had a unique brass section with Little Benny Bailey, Dizzy Gillespie, Gayle Brochan, and Parker—these gentlemen played arranged modern lines that were not limited to the unison lines used by other bands. Dizzy and Tadd Dameron would orchestrate Dameron's lines and clichés for the horn players and "rejuvenated the band" by spurring soloists to find even fresher ways to play. And then there was Bird. If blues tonality and improvisational panache distinguishes twentieth-century American music from the rest of Western music, then Charles Parker was arguably the greatest instrumentalist America has produced. His execution was faster, cleaner, and more rhythmically complex than was even imaginable by most players. And his technique, as dazzling as it was, never outstripped the quality and clarity of his ideas. He had the best diatonic ear, and though he died young (thirty-six), he wrote the book on how to improvise through the diatonic system as much as Bach, four centuries earlier, had codified harmonic modulation and other diatonic compositional devices.

As a young artist, Miles was attentive to all the details presented to him. Speaking about Billy "Mr. B." Eckstine's band, he said, "I knew all the parts, looked at the arrangements, studied the chords. I was in school." It was playing on the street, and with Parker, more so than attending Juilliard that represented a sort of postgraduate study for Miles. What Davis learned from the musicians on 52nd Street would stay with him throughout his life and career.

It wasn't long before Davis officially left Juilliard. His real education was happening on the bandstands and in the clubs, while his father had been paying his tuition and providing him with a stipend. Davis recalled telling his father, " 'It is a white school, everything is white, the concept is white. Everything is changing.' I told him about Diz and Bird." His father supported his decision to leave. By 1945, Juilliard was behind him.

John Szwed writes, "Creativity such as Parker's and Gillespie's happens maybe once in a lifetime. Miles and Freddie Webster were well aware of the level and speed of the innovation in front of them and brought music manuscript paper along with them to the club every night to jot down whatever Dizzy was playing (Parker was too fast to transcribe, Miles said), and when the paper ran out, they wrote on matchbook covers and napkins . . . bebop was . . . a scholarly enterprise that required intelligence and commitment, and Miles thrived on it."[1] In addition to his association with these two giants, Davis began to play with the inestimable Thelonious Monk, as well as with Max Roach and Bud Powell.

On November 26, 1945, Davis recorded with Parker for the first time. The Savoy Records release was also Bird's first recording as leader. They recorded "Billie's Bounce," "Now's the Time," and "Thriving on a Riff." Although some critics say that Miles's performance on these sides is weak, the recording provides evidence to the contrary. In fact, it might even be said that he affects Bird's performance. Miles's playing is strong here and already shows his unique conception. The three recordings, all Parker originals, are based on the mainstay of bebop compositions. The first two, "Billie's Bounce" and "Now's the Time," are blues in F, and the third, "Thriving on a Riff," is based on "rhythm changes" in B-flat. So the forms are familiar and the keys are stock keys, so to speak. Today, most aspiring jazz musicians learn to play the blues in F and the rhythm changes in B-flat very early in their careers, and more tunes are written over those two forms, often in those two keys, than any others in jazz.

"Billie's Bounce" is interesting because of the relaxed manner in which Bird plays his four-chorus solo. Maybe this is in honor of Billie Holiday's relaxed phrasing, but it could also be the result of Miles's melodic influence. Bird's complex rhythmic virtuosity is always evident, and he usually has several long passages of double timing (places where the soloist phrases in rhythmic values that are twice as fast as usual—sixteenth notes instead of eighths, though with Bird the acceleration could be even faster). In this solo, there is only one such passage, given briefly on the last phrase of the second chorus. Miles-like, he starts his fourth chorus with long sustained notes and retains the relaxed eighth-note phrasing throughout the solo. Miles takes only two choruses, continuing the relaxed feeling that Parker evokes. His bebop credentials are evident in his wry emphasis on the tritone at the end of his first phrase. His penchant for the unusual is found in the following silence, right at the part where you would expect the second idea or phrase to begin.

"Now's the Time" is another blues in F; however, the listener is not in the least bored because the tune is arranged and played so differently. This song is an important recording for a number of reasons: First is its political connotation, suggesting the militancy and postwar expectations of black Americans. No more waiting; *now* is the time. Second, the same melody was recorded as an R&B hit, "The Hucklebuck," by Paul Williams. The emergence of bebop was the beginning of a new kind of African American modernism, one that diverged, if only slightly, from the popular tastes of everyday black folk. By the 1960s, not only did bebop music have the distinction of being one of the most sophisticated and intellectually challenging musics in the world, it was also one of the first African American musics that was not explicitly dance music. At this juncture of jazz history, rhythm and blues emerged as the vernacular music to which black folks danced. That one of Bird's most significant blues compositions was also an R&B hit suggests that this bifurcation between the two musics was not inevitable; nor was playing R&B anathema according to the practices of bebop's greatest practitioner. In the late 1940s, jazz musicians and R&B musicians shared a vocabulary and used the same musical forms, often crossing boundaries between the two. Both Parker and Louis Jordan (the star R&B saxophonist/vocalist who had apprenticed in Chick Webb's orchestra) played blues and rhythm changes more than any other form. Bird and Dizzy both recorded with Tiny Grimes, a jazz guitarist who was also a pioneer of rock and roll. Neither Parker nor Gillespie was by any means what we would today call a jazz purist. Albert Murray writes that when the Count Basie Orchestra (one of the greatest dance bands) came around, there were hipsters who would crowd the bandstand primarily to listen, not to dance, paying special attention to Lester Young. And the Lindy Hoppers found ways to dance to the complicated rhythms of bebop. Of course, Davis would later emerge as one of the most important crossover artists in jazz's history when he fomented the electronic revolution in jazz during the 1960s and 1970s. Here in his first recording with the great Charlie Parker, they record a blues that would exemplify the common ground between bebop and the more dance-oriented popular music.

As in the other twelve-bar blues on the album, it is possible that Dizzy Gillespie is on piano. Sadik Hakim was also in the studio ready to play, but he was unable to do so while the union representative was there because he did not have a union card. He did play once the representative left, but it is unclear which takes were used. The piano introduction, played in a call-and-response pattern with the bass (played by Curly Russell), is intriguing and not necessarily suggestive of a blues.

Dizzy's presence on the date is significant. When the world's greatest bebop trumpeter was also on the date, why would Bird, or anyone, use Miles if his playing was not up to par or if he were not able to articulate Parker's musical ideas? No matter what the critics say about his performance on this recording, the musicians have given Miles's solo an emphatic thumbs-up. First, Eddie Jefferson's vocalese version of "Now's the Time" (1959), ostensibly a paean to Parker, includes Miles's solo right after Bird's, just as it occurs on the recording. Vocalese tributes to jazz masters have immortalized specific solos, most famously James Moody's solo on "Moody's Mood for Love" (the vocalese version, written and conceptualized by Jefferson, was recorded by King Pleasure in 1952) but also those of other important musicians, including Bird, Miles, and others. Also, thirteen years later, in 1958, when Miles records *Milestones* along with Coltrane and company, he plays a blues in F, this time penned by Monk, "Straight, No Chaser." On that recording, Red Garland's solo pays tribute to Miles's earlier efforts on the F blues. He replays Miles's entire solo from "Now's the Time" at the end of his own improvisation, voicing the trumpeter's lines in block chords.

The third tune recorded, "Thriving on a Riff," begins not with a melody, but with Miles Davis improvising. Bird was fond of this device, as is evident on "Relaxing with Lee," "Bird of Paradise," and other Parker recordings. Interestingly, it is Miles and not Bird who starts off here. Again, this would have been a great deal of responsibility for a young musician who was not cutting the mustard. Miles executes the solo admirably, justifying Bird's trust in his ability to do so. At the end of the track, Bird and Miles play the head, which would later become known as "Anthropology." Together, these three recordings attest to Miles's musical competence and promise. The young musician met the standard set for him by his idol. Miles had been accepted by his elders as one of the most important trumpeters in the music. That he was able to use the bebop vocabulary without sounding like Dizzy marked him as special indeed. This ability to find his own way and to stand apart from the bravura style so common among trumpeters would forever be part of his artistic reputation.

When Parker and Gillespie went to Hollywood for eight weeks in December 1945 to introduce their music to West Coast audiences, Davis returned to East St. Louis to visit family for the holidays and then hooked up with Benny Carter's big band, also headed for Los Angeles—the band's base. While in Los Angeles, bored by the Carter band's swing arrangements, Davis ventured to late-hour jam sessions, where he met West Coast–based musicians like Red Callender, Art and Addison Farmer, and Charles Mingus. After leaving Carter for good by the fall of 1946, Davis stayed in Los Angeles until he received notice that Irene was once again expecting. Needing money to return to East St. Louis, he replaced Fats Navarro in Billy Eckstine's band and traveled as far as Chicago with them.

While playing gigs in Los Angeles with Benny Carter and in Chicago with Billy Eckstine, Davis began to use drugs more regularly. According to Miles, he first tried cocaine in Billie Holiday's dressing room in early 1945 when he replaced Joe Guy in Coleman Hawkins's band. He continued with different forms of cocaine while on the road with Eckstine but eventually began to use heroin with saxophonist Gene Ammons. (Ammons later spent eleven years in prison because of his drug use.) When Davis returned to New York, his regular use of heroin was not immediately evident. He was still able to maintain family life with Irene, Cheryl, and their new baby boy, Gregory.

The following year, Davis rejoined Parker in New York in April 1947, replacing Gillespie. The Gillespie/Parker collaboration had set the musician community on fire. If Dizzy was slightly less inventive melodically than was Bird (*everybody* was less inventive than Bird), he was revered for his encyclopedic knowledge of bebop. He taught piano players how to voice the new music, he taught drummers how to accompany the new rhythms, and he was a leading composer and arranger for bop bands of all sizes. His genius for projecting his musical ideas and charisma onstage, along with the business acumen of his wife, Lorraine, helped to make Gillespie the public face of bop. He also possessed a brilliant technique, being able to play incredibly fast, intricate, harmonically sophisticated ideas in all registers of the trumpet.

It was difficult for the younger Davis to step into Gillespie's shoes. At the time, he had neither the range nor the pyrotechnics that Gillespie took for granted. But he did have a unique and warm tone as well as a true gift for lyricism. Davis added a melodic beauty to the bop idiom that few have ever matched. On the sides that he created with Parker, he can be heard carving out his own niche in the music, not imitating Dizzy or Bird. The results are fantastic. And the recordings of this particular band are among the most melodic that Parker ever made. "Moose the Mooche" and especially "Yardbird Suite," both Parker compositions, are but two examples. Miles's lyrical approach provided a contrast to the busy nature of Parker's lines. As a bandleader, Davis eventually found a similar contrasting balance between his voice and the more bombastic tenor sax of Coltrane.

The summer of 1947 found Coleman Hawkins in residence at the Three Deuces, a New York jazz club. Thelonious Monk was the piano player, and Miles tried to sit in as often as possible. Monk became his tutor. It was Parker who first introduced Miles to Monk. Miles would also see him at Minton's, the renowned Harlem nightspot where the architects of bebop began their experimentations. In addition to Bird and Monk, Kenny Clarke, Bud Powell, Dizzy Gillespie, and Max Roach— a veritable *Who's Who* of modern jazz—were frequently there. It was the place where musicians could go after their regular jobs and relax while experimenting with new ideas amid friendly competition. Miles later said that the air there was "electric," that people would jockey for a chance to sit in where the pianist/composer held court at the piano chair. Monk was also a regular at Gillespie's home, where Miles, Max Roach, Bird, and others would meet to discuss, study, and practice music. Monk was an iconoclast, playing what Miles called "spacey shit" with unusual chord voicings. Later, he would say of first hearing Monk playing on 52nd Street and at Minton's, "His use of space in his solos and his manipulation of funny-sounding chord progressions just knocked me out, fucked me up. I said, 'Damn, what is this motherfucker doing?' Monk's use of space had a big influence on the way I played solos after I heard him."[2]

After Gillespie convinced him of the importance of learning the piano in order to recognize the right tensions to play with the new harmonies, Miles persuaded Monk to write out chords for him. Davis seems to have learned a great deal from Monk: The latter's sense of space is as unusual as that of Miles and is definitely one of the models for it. Both artists were unique among the bebop generation in their willingness to make long silences part of their melodic statements. One of the things that results from their timing is that a single note can take on greater poignancy than is available to another artist's flurry of notes. Often a brief gesture by either of these two artists is pregnant with emotion and feeling as well as harmonic, melodic, and rhythmic insinuation.

In a music in which every player worth his or her salt strives for originality, Monk's playing stood out from that of even the most creative improvisers. His sense of style was modern, and he was one of the main architects of the music during its incubation at Minton's in Harlem. His style was also rooted in older musics; as a teenager he toured the country, playing for a revivalist. Monk was also influenced by the Harlem stride pianists and by Duke Ellington. But the ways that he navigated these various streams of music were as unusual as his name. He often truncated his ideas, leaving gaping holes in the melodies, while at other times he would produce long, arabesque figures peppered with tonal clusters and long runs covering as many as six octaves. Miles credits Monk with teaching him more about composition than anyone else on 52nd Street.

During the period when both played with Hawkins, Monk showed Davis chords and voicings. Hawkins was one of the few musicians of his generation who routinely worked with the younger progressive musicians. He was universally regarded as the "father" or the "inventor" of the saxophone. It was not Adolphe Sax, the Belgian instrument maker and inventor, but Hawk who first realized its full potential as a singing instrument capable of virtuosic statements. He became even more legendary when, after living as an expatriate in Europe, he returned to the States in 1939 and cut his megahit "Body and Soul." His solo on that recording has been studied by every generation of saxophonists from then until now.

Davis would ask nightly whether he played Monk's "Round Midnight" correctly, and only after many tries did he perform it successfully enough to garner the composer's approval. Getting it right meant soloing in such a manner as to allow the melody (and not just the harmonies) to be heard simultaneously. Monk, of course, was quite fond of using the melodies and paraphrases of the melodies in his own improvisations. Miles's version of "Round Midnight," recorded with John Coltrane for Columbia in 1955, shows just how much Miles learned from this. His reading of the melody is so dramatic and rich that his performance dominates the others' even though he does not solo on the cut and Coltrane takes what is widely regarded as his first masterful solo on a record. It is probably also the most famous and listened-to version of the song, more memorable than even the composer's versions.

On August 14, 1947, Davis fronted his own band and recorded his first session as leader, but the record, currently issued as *Miles Davis All Stars,* was recorded for Savoy and released under Bird's name. Then, as now, record companies were more interested in marketing than in representing the session accurately. Even today you can buy this record as *Bird on Tenor* because of the sales such a title might generate.

In the fall of that year, Davis joined Trummy Young, Sonny Stitt, Lucky Thompson, Sarah Vaughan, Ray Brown, Milt Jackson, and Tadd Dameron in the annual *Esquire's Jazz Book* of 1947 as a "New Star." The *Esquire* annuals were very important to the musicians and their fans. For the former, they were great promotional tools—musicians did not necessarily land specific jobs because of the annuals, but appearing in them increased their prestige and name recognition, which could translate into larger audiences and more engagements. As an aspiring player in St. Louis, Davis used to stare at photos of his idols in the *Esquire* annuals and dream of joining them in New York. However, his own appearance in the magazine was bittersweet. Although the poll recognized the talent of a number of younger musicians and thus the music they were creating, the overall volume featured privileged visual images of white musicians and articles about earlier forms of the music. Ernest Anderson, a promoter who worked closely with the white jazz guitarist Eddie Condon, had edited the 1947 book. The Harlem-based African American newspaper, the *Amsterdam News,* reported:

> The book . . . carries thirty-seven photos of white musicians with only seventeen Negro musicians and singers. At least twenty of the pictures of the musicians {are} with the Eddie Condon outfit. . . . There is a series of about twenty pictures of the Condon group in an eight-page spread and not a single Negro face appears among them. It reeks of "Dixieland" and "white supremacy music."

A letter was written and addressed to David Smart, *Esquire*'s publisher, protesting the volume's treatment of black musicians and of the more modern forms of jazz. It is worth quoting at length:

> We, *a group of musicians who have won awards in the Esquire All American Jazz Polls, hereby protest against the treatment given to the poll in* Esquire's 1947 Jazz. We wish to know the answers to the following: Why was the book edited by the personal manager of Eddie Condon, who has nothing to do with jazz today, and why did it devote much of its space to publicity stories and pictures of musicians who work for Condon and for the editor? . . . Why does the list of the year's so-called best records ignore practically every record made by the younger jazz musicians including the Esquire *winners, while devoting most of its space to records made by older musicians of the Dixieland clique?*

We regard the entire book as an insult to the musical profession and to the jazz musicians who have helped Esquire *by taking part in its jazz activities.*

As long as the present unfair set-up continues, we do not wish to vote in any future polls, and we will refuse to accept any future awards.[3]

The letter was signed by a number of jazz luminaries, including most of the members of Duke Ellington's band as well as Louis Armstrong, Coleman Hawkins, Roy Eldridge, Red Norvo, Buddy Rich, Dizzy Gillespie, Flip Phillips, Pete Candoli, Shadow Wilson, Tadd Dameron, Sarah Vaughan, Billie Holiday, Buck Clayton, Oscar Pettiford, Teddy Wilson, Ella Fitzgerald, Duke Ellington, Ray Nance, Nat "King" Cole, and, just left of center, in between Holiday and Casey, Miles Davis. Two things are interesting about this list: It is racially integrated, and the signers are not just from the younger generation, but representative of the living history of the music itself. Furthermore, the letter itself never mentions race. It doesn't have to.

John Szwed writes that the signatories were "objecting to what they saw as a reactionary and Jim Crow view of their music."[4] The spirit of organized protest, which characterized much of black America's response to racism, is evident in the letter. The African American musicians who signed the letter were not simply grateful to have had a modicum of recognition. They insisted on the respect they deserved. The white musicians among them were part of a community far more integrated than mainstream society, and they, too, were committed to a different racial vision for their country.

Following this incident, there were to be no more annual *Esquire* jazz books. Legendary critic and promoter Leonard Feather wrote that the incident "marked the end of the *Esquire* era."[5]

In agreeing to sign the letter, Davis revealed a part of himself that would surface as a dominant characteristic of his public persona. He was a talented artist whose accomplishments would be honored and recognized. He was also a black man who refused to quietly accept what he thought of as a racist slight. It is important to remember Davis's youth throughout this period: In 1947, he was only twenty-one years old.

Shortly after settling his young family in a Queens apartment, he continued to study the music on his own and to play with Parker. He took advantage of all the cultural options available to him in New York, including attending classical music concerts and even "going to see Martha Graham dance to John Cage's music."[6] The abundance and variety of creative activity available to him in New York had to have been inspiring and stimulating. All through his life, Davis would both appreciate and participate in a variety of art forms.

Through the next two years, he continued to tour and record with Parker, but he began to grow weary of Parker's drug-induced antics and irresponsibility. Getting paid after the gig could be an ordeal; at times, Bird was paid per set rather than per night. This practice was otherwise nonexistent. Bands were (and are) almost always paid nightly, sometimes weekly. Bird was paid by the set to ensure that he would stay for the entire gig. Often Parker would have to borrow a horn

(Jackie McLean once spoke of having to accompany Bird to the gig when he loaned him his horn to make sure he got it back). While at the Three Deuces, there was a man assigned to procuring and, after the gig, repawning a saxophone for Bird. Miles began thinking about quitting Bird's band when on a particularly bad night the band encountered some "redneck-cracker shit" in Indianapolis. A fight broke out between the hooligans and Max Roach and Miles. After that fight, Bird added insult to injury by claiming he couldn't pay the band. While Max accepted Bird's excuse, Miles hunted Parker down, "picked up a beer bottle and broke it and with it poised in my hand said to Bird, 'Motherfucker, give me my money or I'm gonna kill you.' "[7] Reportedly, Bird made light of the matter but nevertheless paid Miles his salary.

Miles was also in search of new musicians and different in-strumental arrangements for his playing. By the end of 1947, he met the man who would help provide that setting, Gil Evans. At the time, Evans was known primarily as an arranger. In the 1930s, he'd started a big band based in Stockton, Cali-fornia. By the early 1940s, he'd become the chief arranger for the Claude Thornhill Orchestra. By the time he and Miles be-gan to collaborate, Evans had gained the respect of critics as well as other musicians. His 55th Street apartment became a gathering place for a number of younger musicians, including Gerry Mulligan and Lee Konitz. In Evans, Davis found a mu-sical soul mate; the two worked together to form Miles's first legendary group, the Miles Davis Nonet, which included Gerry Mulligan (baritone sax), Max Roach (drums), and John

Lewis (piano). In September 1948, the band had a two-week stint at the Royal Roost (nicknamed the Metropolitan Bopera House).

This residency was important for the nonet. Prior to this, it had been only a rehearsal band, not a performing unit. The nonet was highly unusual in that it was an arranger's band (including not only Gil Evans, but Gerry Mulligan and John Lewis). In spite of the fact that it was an arranger's band, Miles nonetheless seemed to dominate. Mulligan attributes his dominance to his ability to secure them gigs. However, recorded evidence also reveals him to be hands down the most compelling improviser; Mulligan asserted that "without his input we may have forgotten these recordings, good as they are."

Following that first stint, the band often played at the Royal Roost throughout 1948. The Royal Roost (originally a chicken restaurant) was owned by Ralph Watkins. The music there was modern; Tadd Dameron's tentet (in which Miles sometimes played) was the house band, and around the time that the nonet appeared there, both Basie's and Bird's bands played there as well. Miles put the arrangers' names on a sign out front, giving them a newfound prominence. This was an unusual move, especially for jazz, an art form in which the arrangers are hardly ever acknowledged, let alone glorified. Basie listened every night and thought the music was good, if strange. This seems to be the general opinion of the musicians who came down. But the fact that it was a little different was a selling point for the musicians, and the musicians came out to hear the band. The gigs were exciting for Miles, who was beginning to find his voice. He realized that his own music could be less intense than Bird's, and Gil Evans's subtle voicings helped him realize how to showcase his ideas. The audiences were sparse, but Pete Rugolo, an arranger for the Stan Kenton Orchestra (a big band that also featured innovative arranging) and also the musical director for Capitol Records, was in attendance. So although the nonet did not get a lot of gigs out of their residency, they did get to pull it together in front of Rugolo, who then got Capitol to sign Miles.

In January 1949, the nonet went into the studio to record four single records for Capitol. In April, they returned for another session, this time recording "Venus de Milo," "Boplicity," "Rouge," and "Israel." And in March 1950, the same group returned to the studio yet again. Eventually, in 1954, eight of the recordings would be released on a ten-inch LP titled *Birth of the Cool,* and in 1957, a twelve-inch record would be released that included three additional songs.

The *Birth of the Cool* sessions would be historic. Although the band never really became a force as a performing entity, the recording proved to be influential. The careers of Mulligan and Evans blossomed from this point forward. Evans would go on to make other large-scale recording projects with Miles, all of which were financial and artistic successes. Mulligan, who was one of the main arrangers for the sessions, would build on this cool aesthetic and become a pioneer with his pianoless quartet. Most important, *Birth of the Cool* showcased Miles as a major innovator. Playing second horn to Charles Parker had placed him in the limelight, to be sure, but with this recording

Miles is front and center as the most significant improviser on the date. And the hip arrangements with their unusual forms and divisions between arranger and improviser threw the ball over the plate, where Miles liked it best. Hitting home run after home run, he could no longer be compared disparagingly to Dizzy Gillespie. Miles's authority as an improviser was evident, and he would determine the settings for his music from this point on.

As a nonet, the *Birth of the Cool* band was unusual in size: Most of the modern jazz bands were quintets or an occasional big band. (The groundbreaking bop big bands of Hines, Eckstine, and Gillespie were artistically very important but economic failures.) When the usual quintet format (rhythm section plus two horns, usually playing in unison, on the front line) was augmented by a horn or two, the musical format did not necessarily change. Instead of an octet, for instance, the band might sound like a quintet plus three. However, Davis's nonet was more like a small big band than an expanded quintet. The band and the arrangements (written mostly by Evans and Mulligan) were modeled after the innovative Claude Thornhill Orchestra, which preceded the nonet. Thornhill's group differed from the regular big band pattern of alternating sections of reeds and brass set by Don Redman and Fletcher Henderson in the 1920s. Only Ellington's band was as irregular in its use of the different sections of the orchestra. And the components of the orchestra utilized different instrumentation, favoring a dark, mellower sound than was standard for big bands. Thornhill's was probably the most creative of the white big bands: He used the Ellington technique of featuring soloists for passages within a written arrangement (which Evans used to great effect with Miles), hired clarinetists who played only clarinet (and all of his saxophonists doubled on clarinet), hired French horns, and rearranged European art music for jazz audiences.[8] Rather than the improvisational voice of the particular instrumentalists (Miles was the lead soloist), the chief value of each instrument was the way it added color to the orchestration and arrangement. The orchestration was unusual for jazz—there was a tuba and a French horn, but no tenor saxophone. The arrangements were thoughtful and subtle, softer than the usual big band fare. There were no fanfares or shout choruses with blasting brass. The songs were also novel in that the solo passages and the ensemble passages parried back and forth in unusual patterns, sticking to neither thirty-two-bar song cycles or, for that matter, eight-bar phrasing.

The album also exhibited most of the hallmarks of what came to be called "cool jazz." Where bebop was hot and frenetic in tempo and timbre, cool jazz was more laid-back and less blues inflected in its overall expression. In a culture that often contrasts emotional effusiveness with intelligence and control, there was a danger of ignoring the intellectual achievement of the beboppers in favor of the cool school of jazz. The tendency to exaggerate this supposed difference was no doubt exacerbated by the fact that cool jazz was racially coded as "white" while bebop was coded as "black."

With *Birth of the Cool,* Davis became one of the founding

architects of a new school of jazz. Cool jazz was based upon modern music, the name by which the beboppers called their music. Certainly cool players did not ignore the harmonic advances of bebop, but, like Miles, they strove for increased lyricism and often played at a less frenetic pace. As a rule, their playing was less blues inflected and less rhythmically dense than bebop and the hard bop that emerged in the mid-1950s as a response to cool. While many heard less intensity in the cool school when compared with the boppers, this was not always the case: Lennie Tristano's music, with its intensity and complicated melodies, is one example. In general, however, the "cool" musicians were staid in comparison with the other proponents of modern music.

The cool school, especially the wing known as West Coast jazz, was also identified by white musicians and audiences as a movement to assert the dominance of white musicians in response to bebop, which had been pioneered by black musicians. As the popularity of bebop waned, black audiences began dancing to rhythm and blues and doo-wop music. They would not return to jazz in large numbers until the advent of hard bop. Indeed, many of the cool school players graduated from white big bands such as those led by Woody Herman and Stan Kenton. While it is true that many of the most prominent cool musicians were white, there were black leading figures as well: Chico Hamilton, John Lewis, and the Modern Jazz Quartet (MJQ). And of course, Davis's cool trumpet stylings were imitated widely by white trumpeters such as Shorty Rogers and Chet Baker. Another black model for the cool school was "the President," Lester Young, who was the first saxophonist to bring to the fore a light, dry tone, with an emphasis on lyrical swinging rather than harmonic exploration. Prez's influence is especially noticeable in the tenor saxophonists, such as Stan Getz and Zoot Sims. But most cool players, such as Lee Konitz and Wayne Marsh, show considerable sympathy with the harmonies of bop.

The Birth of Cool was a critical and commercial success; however, Davis, ever the restless artist, had already moved on long before the complete recording finally reached the public in 1957. By the time of its release, Miles was well into the formation of his quintet with Trane and Philly Joe. Along with the Jazz Messengers and the Clifford Brown & Max Roach Quintet, Miles's new group was self-consciously black and deliberately hot.

At the end of the 1940s, Davis performed at the first Paris Jazz Festival, where he enjoyed star status. The festival featured a full roster of jazz luminaries, including Sidney Bechet, Charlie Parker, Hot Lips Page, and Leadbelly. As was the case with a number of African American artists and intellectuals, in Paris Davis found appreciation for his art and a sense of freedom from American racial stereotypes (unlike a number of others, he doesn't seem to have made any public statement about France and its contentious relationship to its own colored folk). Miles later recalled that in France, "the horns sound different, the drums sound different. Bird was there. Sidney Bechet was there. Juliette and I used to walk all over Paris." Although the United States had only recently fought and won a war that in many ways challenged notions of white supremacy, black Americans were still second-class citizens, engaged in an ongoing domestic struggle against American racial apartheid. One of the most obvious aspects of that social order was the continued restrictions placed on interracial romance.

In France, for the first time, Miles found these strictures on interracial relationships relaxed. He met and fell in love with French actress Juliette Greco even while Irene and their two children were back in New York. Of falling in love with Greco, Davis said, "I never felt like that in my life." It was his first mature love affair. "In St. Louis I was so busy learning music, I never had time for that." Miles was probably inexperienced with women, especially compared with most traveling jazz musicians. In St. Louis, his sexual knowledge had been limited to Irene, his first girlfriend. Miles believed that the artistic ambitions of a lot of musicians had been ruined by marrying the first girl they impregnated. Miles never married Irene, however, and he certainly didn't let his relationship with her get in the way of his career or his romantic attachments, for that matter.

His affair with Greco would continue in starts and stops over several years after a beginning that was almost a storybook romance in the City of Lights. Though unable to speak each other's languages, in one week they established a bond that time, distance, and other lovers would not diminish. With Greco he entered into an elite circle of artists and intellectuals, including Jean-Paul Sartre and Pablo Picasso. That community wanted him to marry Greco and stay in Paris. But he chose to return to the States.

With a new sense of himself as an artist, Davis returned— only to be confronted by America's postwar recession, continued racism, and his ever burdensome family responsibilities. "I couldn't say nothing when I came back, I was too motherfucking depressed," he said later.

Although he had so far managed to stay away from the full-blown addictions that plagued a number of brilliant musicians, Davis became addicted to heroin. He wasn't alone. Parker, Art Blakey, Billie Holiday, Bud Powell, Tadd Dameron, Dexter Gordon, Gerry Mulligan, and a number of others were caught up in the heroin epidemic of post–World War II urban centers. According to historian Eric Schneider, heroin began to dominate the urban drug trade in the years following World War II and quickly became the drug of choice among black and Puerto Rican youth. Schneider notes that jazz clubs sustained a prewar marijuana subculture that eventually gave way to heroin use. Schneider writes: "Marijuana smoking was relatively benign, but its users were primed to disregard official and media-generated alarms about drugs, which, according to their experience, had little basis in reality. And they traveled in an underground social setting in which one drug fad could easily give way to another."[9] World War II cut off many of the heroin trade routes; but after the war, the number of heroin users, specifically in New York, rose tremendously, and the jazz clubs that had been the site of much of the marijuana subculture also became the site of heroin sales, distribution, introduction, and use. Many of the well-known clubs on 52nd Street, popularly known as Swing Street, were certainly such sites. Stories abound about the relationship between addicted musicians, club owners who did little to discourage drug dealers, and managers who supplied drugs as a means of controlling the artists. In many cases, those same managers would turn their clients in to the authorities when the artists did not act according to their bidding. This is not to suggest that there was a great overarching conspiracy, merely a conflation of social factors that contributed to the epidemic. Perhaps more important, in some circles of jazz musicians, heroin use became part of the lifestyle, a practice of the "in," hip crowd, and the most significant producers of the new music. Parker, the most revered of the modern musicians, was famously addicted to heroin, a fact that led some young aspirants to emulate his habit, thinking it might improve their creativity and credibility.

Eventually, the dark side of addiction caught up with Davis, and the once professional, stylish, beautiful young man with a horn was missing gigs, nodding off, and generally unreliable. He began to demonstrate all the junkie tendencies that would jeopardize his reputation. He also lost his family. By 1950, he'd separated from Irene because heroin took priority. In August of that year, Davis and Art Blakey were arrested for possession of narcotics. After spending one night in jail, Davis was released, and at the trial that followed, the jury decided in his favor. However, because the arrest made the newspapers and jazz publications, he found it more and more difficult to get work. As he struggled to rid himself of this chemical dependency, he accepted stints on the West Coast and in Detroit, where he was known as a notorious junkie but one who still had his chops and could silence a room with the soulfulness of his sound.

According to Davis, his habit snuck up on him. Thinking he had a cold or the flu, Davis had no idea that he was instead experiencing symptoms of withdrawal. An acquaintance informed him that he had a habit; the observation proved to be true when, upon snorting heroin, Davis immediately began to feel better. The acquaintance recommended he begin to shoot the drug for quicker relief.

In 1951, in the midst of this chaos, Bob Weinstock, founder of Prestige Records, gave Davis an advance of $750 cash to record for his label. Prestige was one of the small independent labels that found success by recording bop musicians when the major labels wouldn't touch them. Founded by Weinstock in 1949, the label recorded artists like Wardell Gray, Thelonious Monk, and Stan Getz. Engineer Rudy Van Gelder recorded many of the Prestige sessions in the company's Hackensack, New Jersey, studio.

Over the years, Prestige developed a reputation for issuing cash advances to many of its drug-addicted artists. According to some musicians, the company often paid little and issued manipulative contracts to musicians desperate for cash. Advances were set against future royalty payments, and royalties were low. Saxophonist Jackie McLean also signed with Prestige, a decision he later regretted:

> *I was starving when I signed that contract. The baby was being born, so I was glad to get my name on a record and make some money. And my condition {as a heroin addict} didn't help either. . . . Everybody made that move—Miles was with that company, Sonny Rollins, John Coltrane, and Monk. They all got out of it as soon as they could, just as I did.*

Of Prestige's exploitative practices, John Szwed writes, "It was business as usual, only worse."

Later, in the mid-1950s, Davis "advised younger musicians just arriving in New York to contract with any other company save Prestige."[10] It is little wonder Davis constantly requested that Columbia Records producer George Avakian buy him out of the Prestige contract and sign him to Columbia. Avakian would avoid doing so until he was sure Davis was no longer addicted to heroin. Consequently, Davis's habit not only interfered with his performance and family life, but also jeopardized his recording career and made him vulnerable to unscrupulous businessmen.

Davis returned to East St. Louis in an attempt to kick his habit. His sister Dorothy told his father that the beloved son was a drug addict. Dr. Davis told him: "If it was a woman, you could tell me and I'd tell you to get another woman, but this you have to do on your own." At different times he had his son arrested, and he even drove him to a sanatorium in Lexington,

Kentucky, where addicts went to recover. However, Miles refused to commit himself. During the years of his addiction, he tried to quit on an annual basis. Girlfriends tried to help him; one even took him to talk to a psychiatrist.

Davis later claimed he kicked cold turkey the second time he went to East St. Louis, in November 1953. He said that his effort to get clean took only six days, and he found inspiration in the discipline of boxers like Sugar Ray Robinson. Having been given boxing lessons by his father as a child, he resumed training. The strict physical and mental discipline helped him to combat his cravings for heroin. However, he would not be completely off heroin until the fall of 1954,[11] and he would continue to use cocaine on and off throughout his life.

When Miles returned to New York, free of his addiction, his career took off and he never looked back. He would later recall:

> *Nineteen fifty-four was a great year for me—although I didn't realize how great it was at the time. I had kicked my habit and was playing better than I ever played. . . . I had the feeling that I was getting there, on my own terms. I hadn't compromised my integrity to get to this place of recognition. And if I hadn't done it up to now, then I wasn't going to do it in the future.*[12]

Upon his return to New York in February, just three months before *Brown v. Board of Education,* Davis found a new music scene, dominated by the sound of cool jazz as played by the Modern Jazz Quartet and Dave Brubeck. Brubeck was immensely popular, especially on college campuses, and for many young people he had become the face of jazz. In 1954, Brubeck appeared on the cover of *Time* magazine,[13] becoming the first modern jazz musician to hold the distinction. The cover featured a painted portrait of him, surrounded by white hands playing various instruments; underneath the portrait, the caption reads, "Jazzman Dave Brubeck; the Joints are really Flipping."

In 1953, Davis made *Miles Davis, Vol. 2* for Blue Note, but he had neither a permanent band nor a record contract. Eventually, he signed a three-year deal with Prestige. During this period, Davis became especially impressed with the piano player Ahmad Jamal. Jamal, who hailed from Pittsburgh, was a very compelling musician and bandleader. He differed from most of his contemporaries in a number of ways: As with Miles and Monk, Jamal's style was sparse and subtle and utilized more space than was usual. (At the time, most black musicians were churning out urgent blues-based improvisations.) Unlike Monk, Jamal had a very light touch that Miles also admired. The interplay of Jamal's piano-bass-drums rhythm section was something that Miles found especially exciting. The degree of interplay among the members of his trio and the tightly arranged renditions of his repertoire were especially unusual. Later, Davis would bring his own drummer to hear Jamal's group and to note the way Jamal's drummer, Vernell Fournier, used rim shots on the fourth beat. Jamal's influence on Davis extended down to his choice of repertoire. Miles recorded many tunes from Jamal's book, including "Surrey with the

Fringe on Top," "Just Squeeze Me," "My Funny Valentine," "A Gal in Calico," "Will You Still Be Mine?," "Billy Boy" (which Davis, probably paying homage to Jamal, would record as a piano trio without any horn players), "But Not for Me," and "Ahmad's Blues."

On Christmas Eve that same year, Davis went into the Hackensack studio to record *Miles Davis and the Modern Jazz Giants*. Thelonious Monk was the pianist for this recording session. Although Miles loved Monk's compositions (he recorded "Round Midnight," "Straight, No Chaser," and "Well You Needn't," for instance), he claimed to have hated the way he "comped" (the way he played chords to accompany soloists). During one song, Miles, beyond the point of frustration, finally cursed Monk and demanded that he lay out during his solo. In his autobiography, Miles disavows the famous tale of his argument with Monk while recording the *All Stars of Jazz* album. He states that he and Monk "loved" each other since they had played together with Coleman Hawkins in 1948 on 52nd Street. Besides, Miles contended that Monk was too gentle to have fought him and too big and strong for Miles to survive it had he done so anyway. However, Davis admits that he asked Monk to lay out behind his solos. By having Monk stroll in this way, he achieved the breathing and space in the music that he wanted. Much later, Miles would say he felt that only saxophonists sounded good with Monk's sparse style of comping. It is true that the most legendary interpreters of Monk's music were all virtuosic saxophonists who could play long, "notey" runs. Monk was not known as a bandleader at this time in his career, but in later years he would feature mostly tenor saxophonists, including Coltrane, Sonny Rollins, Johnny Griffin, and especially Charlie Rouse. Trumpet players (who don't "have as many notes"), and especially Miles, who played even fewer notes than most, wanted a different kind of feeling from the piano accompanist. Whatever one thinks of Miles's explanation, it is true that other than Ray Copeland (who was mostly a section player), there are no legendary associations between Monk and trumpet players comparable to those with the above-mentioned saxophonists.

In spite of the drama that allegedly accompanied it, this date produced an extraordinary document of music making among the most astonishing players of the time, including Milt Jackson on vibes, Percy Heath on bass, and Kenny Clarke on drums. Also, according to Davis, "It was on the *Modern Jazz Giants* album that I started to understand how to create space by leaving the piano out and just letting everybody stroll. I would extend and use that concept more later."[14]

In addition to *The Modern Jazz Giants,* Davis released *Walkin'*. According to Davis, Weinstock paid him almost $3,000, a substantial sum at the time, for this album. So the year of his return to New York found him closer to creative and economic freedom than he had ever been: in control of the production of his music and reaping the compensation he deserved. It wasn't a coincidence that he was also free of his heroin addiction.

Walkin' was evidence of the emergence of a new move in jazz—hard bop. On the one hand, hard bop represented a consolidation of the innovations of the modern music movement spearheaded by Bud Powell, Parker, and Gillespie. The basic format was the same as that of modern music/bebop—small combos such as trios and quartets, but especially quintets with trumpet-saxophone front lines, often playing in unison with a piano-bass-drums rhythm section. Like bebop, hard bop used familiar chord progressions, especially blues, but also had a preponderance of melodies in minor keys. Unlike bebop, hard bop was a music that tried to court the connection with its audience (about whom some of the beboppers were nonchalant), especially its black audience. The architects of "modern music" (the bebopper's term for their music) were concerned about their artistic integrity and autonomy in a context where many were ignorant about the sophistication and erudition of black musicians. Because the beboppers had already proven their mettle, the hard boppers did not share this burden. Rather, hard boppers were trying to bring the dance beat orientation, so historically important in black culture, back into the music.

Gone were the abstruse and obscure titles such as Bird's "Anthropology" and "Klactoveesedstene," Monk's "Epistrophy" and "Crepuscule with Nellie." In their place were funky-sounding names that sought to convey the musicians' fluency with the black vernacular such as Bobby Timmons's "Moanin'," "Dis Here," and "Dat Dere" and Nat Adderley's "Work Song." These titles were as everyday in their connotations of dry-longso black life as Louis Armstrong's "Struttin' with Some Barbecue" had been for an earlier generation. Miles was a leader in this regard as well; his first records with the quintet were named and represented orthographically (*Walkin', Workin', Cookin', Relaxin', Steamin'*) in a similar manner. With *Walkin',* Miles stepped into the hard bop fray along with J. J. Johnson, Lucky Thompson, Horace Silver, Percy Heath, and Kenny Clarke. These were sides that later musicians studied for their quintessential hard bop style—deceptively simple, laid-back, and funky, but with all of the harmonic sophistication and instrumental command one could want. "Walkin'" starts with an intro that features a repeated pedal tone in the bass, with the horns playing a simple bluesy melody in unison. The theme itself is a halting melody that brings to mind the motion of someone walking or strolling along. When we get to the solos, the rhythm section plays a blues in F. This is not the harmonically souped-up blues that Charlie Parker and other modern jazzmen would play at times, but the simpler (still jazzy) version of the twelve-bar blues. Horace Silver's two brief choruses are even simpler, lacking the ii-V-I turnaround of the other choruses, just the plain I-IV-V folk blues. Silver's solo is remarkably restrained, with only the slightest hints of the complexity of his thinking; like Miles, he is able to imply whole phrases with a single note. Before the tune's melody returns, there is a two-chorus drum solo accompanied by a riff played by the horns. Again, Kenny Clarke's solo is not the usual flashy, technical display expected of drummers, but subtle interplay between the timekeeping (that he never abandons) and the rhythmic riff of the horns. All of these elements made the music more attractive to a broader black audience and once again helped to initiate yet another style of black music. This music not only swung, it was *funky,* like the urban gait of black men and women or the house parties and dances that they attended.

Although Davis regained his reputation among musicians, produced a number of important albums, and contributed to this new form, it was still difficult for him to get work in clubs because of the reputation he had acquired while addicted to heroin. This would change after the Newport Jazz Festival of 1955. Founded the year before by entrepreneur and jazz impresario George Wein, the Newport Jazz Festival was the first outdoor festival devoted to jazz. It had already become an important venue for artists, audiences, critics, and record company executives. Davis appeared with an all-star band that included Zoot Sims, Gerry Mulligan, Thelonious Monk, Percy Heath, and Connie Kay, who joined them a few songs into the set with "Now's the Time" and Monk's "Round Midnight." On a few tunes Miles played with a mute, which helped to make his sound even more intimate. By the end of the set, Miles had reestablished himself as a unique and individual voice. He recalled: "When I got off the bandstand, everybody was looking at me like I was a king or something—people were running up to me offering me record deals. All the musicians were treating me like I was a god."[15]

George Avakian, producer for Columbia Records, was in the audience that night. Encouraged by the extraordinary Newport performance, and the insistence of his brother, Aram, a filmmaker, photographer, and avid jazz fan, Avakian finally offered Davis a contract. Miles was committed to Prestige, so Avakian began negotiating with Weinstock. Davis recalled, "These motherfuckers were talking about money, real money, so stuff was starting to look good."[16]

Once Weinstock made a deal with Avakian, Davis had the contract and began to organize his band. During a stint at Cafe Bohemia, he featured alto saxophonist Julian "Cannonball" Adderley. Cannonball (a corruption of his childhood nickname, "Cannibal," because of his huge and often indulged appetite) Adderley was the perfect addition to the front line. He was heavily influenced by Parker and had his amazing fluidity and imagination on alto saxophone. Also, like Parker, he had a huge, blues-inflected, happy sound. (Later, he would prove to have enough pyrotechnics to be able to play after John Coltrane and still hold the interest of both audience and musicians without seeming overly tame by comparison.) But at the end of the summer, Adderley returned to Florida to resume his job as a schoolteacher. Davis's drummer, the incomparable Philly Joe Jones, suggested his homeboy, a saxophonist named John Coltrane, replace Adderley. Within days, the Philadelphia-based horn player came to New York to audition for Miles. Recalling the evening at the Audubon Ballroom, Miles was prepared to be unimpressed with Coltrane when the tenor player arrived, but Wallace Roney recalled Miles telling him that Trane made the gig with apparent ease. He was familiar with the repertoire, and for the tunes that he did not know, Miles would discuss the arrangement with him, and off they

went. Miles was newly impressed and within a few days offered Trane the position. In late September 1955, he would
join the band in Baltimore as its newest member.

By 1955, Miles had rid himself of a dependence on heroin;
when Coltrane joined the band in Baltimore that September,
he was still in the throes of his own struggle with the drug.
Apparently, Coltrane began using in 1948. In spite of Philadelphia's well-deserved reputation as a city where drug addicts
were constantly harassed by the police, Coltrane, unlike almost all of his contemporaries, was never arrested. Perhaps his
gentle charm aided him in this. There is an amusing story of
Coltrane and a friend in the bathroom getting high or about to
do so when the cops barge in. They make Coltrane roll up his
sleeves and reveal his tracks. When the policeman points them
out, Coltrane looks at him sincerely with his large, luminous
eyes and declares them to be birthmarks. Remarkably, the cop
bought it.

By all accounts, Coltrane's basic personality was not trans-
formed by his use of the drug; most who knew and interacted
with him recall a sweet, unassuming, and gentle man, as well
as a very talented and disciplined musician. In fact, he maintained many of his southern mannerisms. Unlike Miles, he
wasn't the well-dressed, urban ladies' man. Nor was he a playboy; his attention was devoted primarily to the music. Although the two musicians were close in age, Davis had much
more experience as a professional musician, especially among
the elite ranks of jazz players.

Coltrane had, of course, heard of the dapper trumpeter, and

Miles was also aware of the lesser-known saxophonist at the time of the audition. Coltrane had first come to Miles's attention through the acetate of a performance recorded while he was in the navy in 1946. They may have met shortly thereafter, but Miles recalls first hearing Trane perform live in 1952, when Trane sat in with Miles's band at the Audubon Ballroom (which would later become infamous as the assassination site of Malcolm X). Miles's group that night included Bud Powell, Sonny Rollins, and Art Blakey. It would not have been the first time the two of them met, either. Jimmy Heath recalls introducing Trane to Miles and Bird when Davis and Parker appeared in Philadelphia in the mid-forties, but Miles insisted he first met Trane in Harlem, where he—Miles—was hanging out, chasing music and drugs with Sugar Hill Harlemites Gil Goggins and Jackie McLean and Harlem habitués like Max Roach and Art Blakey.[17] Nonetheless, while they certainly met before the Audubon, that night was the most memorable of their early meetings.

Sitting in was always understood to be the occasional prerogative of qualified musicians. It would not have mattered that Coltrane was not as famous as Miles; he had come up through the ranks and was already a favorite with jazz and R&B stars such as Big Maybelle, Johnny Hodges (Duke Ellington's star lead alto saxophonist and Coltrane's first musical idol), and Dizzy Gillespie.

That night at the Audubon, Trane was no match for Rollins. Perhaps he was simply unfamiliar with the band's book, since he was substituting for Jackie McLean. The presence of two tenors on the bandstand automatically evokes the history of the cutting contest, or musical battle. Legendary battles between the first generation of tenor giants included Lester Young versus Ben Webster and Young versus Coleman Hawkins; later years would witness similar lighthearted, tour-de-force battles between Dexter Gordon and Gene Ammons or the legendary battle between Gordon and Wardell Gray. These couplings were often not really battles at all, just musical collaborations, but the two-tenor format always invites the battle metaphor. Miles would say of the encounter, "Sonny was awesome that night, scared the shit out of Trane, just like Trane would do to him a few years later." Rollins had recorded with Bud Powell and Fats Navarro by 1949, and though he was still a very young man, he had an incredibly mature sound. Even when the two met as stars on *Tenor Madness* in 1956, Sonny debatably had a slight edge over Trane, whose sound and technique would not fully mature for another year or so.

Between that night in 1952 and the time three years later when Coltrane auditioned for Miles's band, Trane had grown tremendously. He'd returned to Philadelphia, where he continued to hone his craft and establish his reputation.

The Philadelphia to which the young Coltrane had migrated in June 1943 was, like New York, a hotbed of jazz music and culture. This was especially so during the years following World War II. The local black newspapers such as the *Philadelphia Tribune* are filled with advertisements, announcements, and articles about the music scene. The city was also the place that nurtured the talents of a young Marian Anderson and served as home base for gospel legends the Clara Ward Singers. There were a number of venues where live jazz could be heard, and the best bands and musicians played in the City of Brotherly Love. Rashied Ali recalls that as a teenager, he and his classmates "used to actually dance to Charlie Parker's music. . . . We used to dance a dance called the 'off time' on Bird's music." And then, one night Parker himself performed at Ali's high school dance!

Coltrane had arrived in the city one month after graduating high school in 1943. At this time, big bands thrived there. Black musicians belonged to the segregated musicians union, and within two years he was a member. He found work playing numerous dances held at places like the O. V. Catto Lodge (named for the nineteenth-century African American activist who was murdered in one of the city's bloodiest race riots) and the Elks Lodge. There were also a number of other clubs and concert halls, not to mention the after-hours spots. According to Coltrane biographer Lewis Porter, the Woodbine Club, at 12th and Master Streets, was not far from Coltrane's initial home at 1450 North 12th Street (between Jefferson and Master).[18] The young musician found himself surrounded by an atmosphere of black music making, especially in the jazz idiom. As noted earlier, after his arrival in Philly his mother gave him an alto saxophone and his new pastor gave him keys to the church so that he could practice without disturbing his neighbors. Although lacking the patronage of a wealthy father like Davis's, Trane nonetheless was surrounded by a supportive community and family who encouraged his pursuits.

By 1944, Coltrane had begun formal training in saxophone and music theory at the Ornstein School of Music in Philadelphia's Center City. There he studied with clarinetist and saxophonist Mike Guerra, who was also a master teacher of contemporary musicians. Guerra said of Coltrane:

> He was easily the best student in my class. I wrote out complex chord progressions and special exercises in chromatic scales, and he was one of the few who brought his homework back practically the next day and played it on sight. It was amazing the way he absorbed everything I gave him. He was always asking for more.[19]

Before long, Coltrane was a member of an exciting group of disciplined, intellectually curious young musicians, including Benny Golson, Jimmy and Percy Heath, and saxophonist Bill Barron, most of whom were on the verge of becoming major contributors to the form.

By 1945, Coltrane was working professional gigs with local musicians. Usually he performed at dances, but he also had the opportunity to play in smaller groups with other musicians who were trying to learn the innovations of bebop.

Like many young men of the time, Coltrane was drafted at the end of World War II, serving approximately one year from August 6, 1945, to August 11, 1946. (Miles would be called for induction in 1954. John Szwed examined military records that demonstrated he failed to report for induction on October 27 and was later dismissed from military service "as an administrative reject.") Following basic training in upstate New

York, Coltrane was sent west to Camp Shoemaker in Northern California, and by late November 1945 he left San Francisco for Oahu, Hawaii—Pearl Harbor. There he started playing in a navy band—the Melody Masters. Unlike white musicians, black navy musicians were not employed as full-time musicians; instead, they had a number of duties besides playing music. As with most black enlisted men in what was still a segregated navy, Coltrane worked primarily on KP or other such menial tasks. Nevertheless, he excelled within these limitations until he was formally discharged.

As a veteran, Trane was eligible for the veterans' benefits of the GI Bill. He took advantage of housing loans and tuition assistance to purchase property for his family and to continue his formal music training. Upon returning to Philadelphia in 1946, he devoted himself entirely to his music. A generation of young musicians, inspired by the innovations of Bird and Gillespie, continued to ensure Philadelphia's reputation as one of the nation's most important jazz cities. Among them were Benny Golson, brothers Bill and Kenny Barron, Lee Morgan, Jimmy and Al "Tootie" Heath, Jimmy Oliver, Odean Pope, McCoy Tyner, Philly Joe Jones, and Red Garland.

During the first couple of years after his return, Coltrane found work with a number of local jazz and rhythm and blues bands, and he went on tour with Joe Web and King Kolax. The King Kolax Band did not play R&B; it was a dance band, but it played mostly instrumental jazz numbers. A big band, it featured a full sax section, trombones, and trumpets as well as a rhythm section. Coltrane played lead alto in the band. In a big band, a saxophonist learns how to blend with section mates, how to breathe and phrase with others. Coltrane seemed to be emulating his first musical idol, Johnny "Rabbit" Hodges, the lead alto player for the Duke Ellington Orchestra, whose beautiful, sinewy sound set the standard for all alto saxophonists until Parker burst on the scene.

The band traveled throughout the States, and Trane learned how to survive on the road. Occasionally, the band would land a weeklong engagement and Coltrane would meet and play with the local musicians. On one occasion, in February 1947, he even played with Charlie Parker while in California. Later, Coltrane would refer to the Kolax band as "my school."[20]

Many a jazz musician has played rhythm and blues—Johnny Griffin, Ornette Coleman, and Julius Hemphill, to name just a few. During his time with Web and Kolax, Trane began to experiment with making lines with the upper tensions of the chords to keep his interest while playing the relatively simple harmonies of R&B tunes. Undoubtedly, another boon to his playing was the need in the R&B idiom for direct communication and a beautiful sound. These were qualities that would continue to serve Coltrane well when his R&B career was over.

One gig in particular was especially important to Coltrane: On tenor, Coltrane joined Eddie "Cleanhead" Vinson's band in late 1948 with a number of other young players, including Red Garland. Coltrane made the switch from alto sax to tenor sax in this band, as Vinson played the alto. While Cleanhead was a showman and a crowd-pleaser, he was also a marvelous saxophone virtuoso. He taught Coltrane "many a trick" while on the road. In one routine, the two saxophonists would switch back and forth between each other's horns, making the necessary key transpositions on the fly.

Trane also played in the big band of Jimmy Heath, who was a member of a prestigious Philadelphia musical family. His brothers, Albert and Percy, made important contributions to the music world on drums and bass, respectively. Jimmy Heath, who has since emerged as one of the most fantastic writers in jazz, was a close friend of Coltrane's during his Philadelphia days. Heath was one of Miles's first choices to fill the tenor chair that Coltrane ended up with in 1955 but was unavailable. As a writer, Heath led a co-op band (they used Jimmy's name, as he was the most well known at the time) in which the two saxophonists worked out their ideas and techniques in the early part of their careers. Heath recalls introducing Coltrane to Davis when Charlie Parker's band played Philadelphia. Like most young musicians, especially saxophonists, Coltrane idolized Parker, and he had the opportunity to play with him when Bird joined the band at a benefit in Philadelphia on December 7, 1947.

During this same period, Coltrane continued both his music training at the Granoff School and frequent visits to the Philadelphia Free Library with Heath. The two listened to Western classical music and studied scores by Stravinsky, among others. In addition to playing alto, Coltrane began playing clarinet. As we have seen, he also began to discover his own voice on tenor:

On alto, Bird had been my whole influence, but on tenor I found there was no one man whose ideas were so dominant as Charlie's were on alto. Therefore, I drew from all the men I heard during this period. I have listened to about all the good tenor men, beginning with Lester, and believe me, I've picked up something from them all, including several who have never recorded.

The reason I liked Lester so was that I could feel that line, that simplicity. My phrasing was very much in Lester's vein at this time.[21]

The first extant recordings made by Coltrane when he was in the navy reveal a developing alto saxophonist trying mightily to imitate Bird. In comparison, all the recordings of him on tenor, throughout his various phases of development, show a player with a highly idiosyncratic approach to improvising and sound production. His tenor sound—hard, metallic, clear, and piercing—was both loved and hated but always considered unique. The willingness to go his own way on tenor may be the single greatest virtue of Coltrane's example as a man and musician.

By September 1949, Coltrane joined Dizzy Gillespie's big band, where he went back to playing alto sax; within a month, Heath joined him. In joining the Gillespie band, Coltrane entered another phase of his musical development. Heath recalled that "Dizzy was a teacher and a giver. He was the most accessible genius I've ever known. Whenever I'd run across him he'd sit me down at the piano and play some voicings and stuff."[22] When Gillespie decided to give up the big band for a smaller ensemble, he retained Coltrane on tenor along with

Milt Jackson on vibes, Percy Heath on bass, Jimmy Heath on alto, Specs Wright on drums, and Fred Strong on conga. But by 1951, Dizzy fired Coltrane and others because of their substance abuse. Trane remained through an engagement at Birdland in New York. Like most addicts, he tried quitting the drug by replacing it with alcohol, a tactic that led to a period of alternating dependencies on heroin and alcohol.

In spite of his personal problems, upon his return to Philadelphia, Coltrane bought a home for himself, his mother, and his cousin Mary and entered the Granoff School of Music to study saxophone and music theory. He resumed working with local R&B bands, where he was expected to be an entertainer as much as an artist. This would include a number of gimmicks like "walking the bar." It was a crowd-pleasing move made especially for the "chitlin circuit."

Walking the bar was a practice that was designed to "take house," or bring in an enthusiastic response from the audience. The saxophonist would not only walk atop the bar while honking and growling through his horn, he would sometimes lie on his back and gyrate his legs while screaming. If the musicians of the bebop generation found the exuberance of Louis Armstrong's performing persona to be Uncle Tom–ish, then walking the bar was seen as not only demeaning, but humiliating. At the same time, there were saxophonists who enjoyed performing to the delight of their audiences and developed the technique with relish. Stripped of its associations with minstrelsy, the ability to connect with African American audiences through this practice of spirited couplings of dance and song, with ecstatic, cathartic expressions, harkened back to sacred ritual in African American song and even further to some African practices as well. Aside from the technical aspects of saxophone playing, the will and ability to connect with audiences on a visceral level through music is a direct connection between these two practices.

Apparently, Coltrane was embarrassed about walking the bar. In one seemingly apocryphal story, Benny Golson arrived in the middle of Coltrane's walking the bar and Coltrane left in embarrassment and didn't return. As with the R&B influence on his playing in general, it is entirely possible that walking the bar set Coltrane's chops and expressive palette for the kind of emotional delivery that became his signature. By the time we get to the movement known as "free jazz" or the "new thing" during the 1960s, the screams and growls that became almost commonplace among saxophonists have a different reception and cultural meaning. As Amiri Baraka demonstrates in his short story "The Screamers," in which saxophonist Lynn Hope plays in such a way as to incite his audience to take mass action on the streets, there may well be a connection between the advanced jazz musician and the "gut bucket" shouter with respect to the reception or at least the meaning of these outbursts. At any rate, Coltrane's shout on the saxophone was as refined within his context as James Brown's vocal shouts were in his, which is saying a lot.

Although Trane did not like the flamboyance of R&B performances, he nonetheless learned a great deal from some of the musicians with whom he worked during this period. In

1952, he toured briefly with alto saxophonist Earl Bostic, who was a popular R&B artist. According to Trane, "I enjoyed it—they had some true music. He's a very gifted musician. He showed me a lot of things on my horn. He has a fabulous technical facility on his instrument and knows many a trick." Lewis Porter speculated that Bostic may have taught Trane how to do circular breathing.[23] After the Bostic gig, Coltrane also toured with Johnny Hodges, his childhood idol, but was again fired for his drug habit. So for the most part he worked in and around Philadelphia, finally ending up with organist Jimmy Smith for a few weeks before he was invited to audition for and then join Miles Davis's band in 1955. His decision to accept this invitation would change the course of his career and the sound of jazz to follow.

Being on the scene in Philadelphia was instrumental in Coltrane getting this opportunity. He was part of a coterie of young musicians who were dedicated to the art and craft of the music. Many of them, like Trane himself, would go on to become legendary musicians. Also, when bandleaders are in search of a new sideman, they will often take suggestions from their existing sidemen, who are usually more connected to rank-and-file musicians. In this case, Miles's drummer and running buddy, Philly Joe Jones, recommended him. Coltrane was nothing if not diligent in his practice regimen and study of music. He had improved greatly since he'd been bested by Rollins and was now ready for the opportunity of his lifetime. No longer would he be in doubt about his ability to sustain himself as a musician. Joining Davis's band would mean steady employment and a high salary. Even more important for Coltrane, it was a chance to grow artistically in a band that maintained high standards while performing almost continuously. For a musician like him, one devoted almost maniacally to the music, this call was a Cinderella-like stroke of luck.

Even so, when asked to join Davis's band, he first said no, protesting that he was in Jimmy Smith's band. According to Roney, Miles had to plead with Trane to get him to say yes. In just a few weeks, he went from living on the good graces of his mother to being able to provide for her as well as start his own family, all this while playing with the top band in the world. There was no doubt that it was the right fit once Trane arrived in Baltimore for the first gig. Some of the tunes he knew; on others, Miles explained the arrangement to him on the spot. Trane's first solo was on the John Lewis composition "Two Bass Hit." Roney relates what Miles told him: "Trane was killing on that first solo. There was no more Sonny for Miles after that. Unlike the critics, Miles never felt that Trane was just developing; he thought that he was bad then, that there was no one better for the gig. He felt that only Bird was a greater saxophonist than Trane."

Although they were of the same generation, by the mid-fifties Miles and Trane were certainly not professional peers. Miles, the precocious trumpeter, had established his reputation as a force to be reckoned with in the jazz world. His peers and elders recognized him as a leading light of his generation, not only as an artist, but as a bandleader as well. He had successfully struggled and won the battle against addiction and was well on his way to garnering an international reputation as a major modern artist. Coltrane, on the other hand, was a late bloomer. A talented and devoted musician, he had not yet hit his stride professionally, nor had he confronted the demons of addiction that continued to haunt him. Nonetheless, he was and would remain a highly disciplined artist committed to reaching his full capacity as a creative being. He had played with leaders as diverse as Vinson and Hodges, but the gig with Miles would change his life. He would grow from a well-respected local musician into an internationally recognized figure who, along with Davis and their band mates, would set the standard for playing jazz. At first he would enter into a relationship with Miles as a kind of apprentice to a master. He would leave as a visionary leader in his own right.

STRUGGLE AND ASCENT

When this group was getting all this critical acclaim, it seemed that there was a new mood coming into the country; a new feeling was growing among people, black and white.

—MILES DAVIS

IN THE SAME YEAR that Miles and Trane joined musical forces, several monumental events brought forth a sense that times were changing, that the nation was leaving behind an era of racial injustice and beginning another era in which it might finally begin to live up to its democratic ideals. Miles Davis's band was made up of young, hip, artistically adventurous men whose music provided a sound track for urban sophistication and signified a refusal to play by the rules. The music echoed the sense of restlessness and determination that seemed to characterize much of America in general and black America in particular in 1955.

The year brought the deaths of Charlie Parker and Emmett Till. Parker's death in March from pneumonia and a bleeding ulcer ended one era in black music history and cleared the way for another. At the time of his death, Bird was not well-known by the general public. Only the hippest listeners were aware of his groundbreaking work. After all, Dizzy Gillespie, not Bird, personified the public face of bebop. But those in the know noted his passing with great sadness: Shortly after Parker's death, graffiti began to appear throughout New York declaring, "Bird Lives!"

And live he did. Thanks to Parker more than any other musician, by the early 1940s, the language of bebop had come to define modern music in the United States. Virtually every established jazz musician since has made Bird's ideas a part of his or her style: His concepts are all staples within mainstream jazz practice today, including rhythmic flow in eighth notes, double-timing passages in sixteenth notes, playing improvised melodies at furiously fast tempos without sacrificing the blueslike cry so important in jazz, structures built upon higher intervals within the chords of a song, and complicated harmonic progressions based on keys descending chromatically or otherwise as a way to structure the blues. The scope of Parker's influence is largely a result of the way he played. With his death there was understandably a profound sense of loss in the musician community. Yet his contributions proved to be lasting and sufficient enough to inspire the next generation of movers and shakers in jazz, including Miles and Trane, both of whom, in a sense, began their innovations where Parker left off.

While Bird's death went with little notice among the general public, the death of Emmett Till captured the emotions of Americans everywhere. His murder, on August 28, 1955, showed that the South was still a very dangerous place for black boys and men. Till, a fourteen-year-old originally from

Chicago but visiting with family in Mississippi, entered Roy Bryant's store with several of his cousins. Bryant was white. A number of the teens dared Till to ask Bryant's wife, Carolyn, on a date. She later testified that Till squeezed her hand and asked, "How about a date, baby?" According to the twenty-one-year-old Mrs. Bryant, after she rebuffed him, Till grabbed her waist and said, "Don't be afraid of me, baby. I ain't gonna hurt you. I been with white girls before." One of Till's cousins recognized the danger of the situation and dragged the young northerner out of the store. Mrs. Bryant charged that Till whistled at her when he left. Within days, Roy Bryant and his cousin J. W. Milam kidnapped Till, beat him to death, and then dumped his body in the Tallahatchie River.

For years, black men had been lynched in Mississippi for alleged infractions against white womanhood, but not since the campaign to free the Scottsboro Boys in the 1930s had an incident generated such an international, multiracial sense of outrage. That Milam and Bryant would be acquitted of their crime asserted that a black man's life was worth little in the American justice system.[1] However, the public reaction to his killing was unique. Scholars and activists now say that Till's murder and his mother's insistence that her boy's brutally beaten and disfigured body be on display in an open casket and in photographs that appeared throughout the black press helped to galvanize the next phase of the black freedom struggle. Few black households were not touched by the Till murder. Naima's daughter, Syeeda, recalls that long after the murder and the case that followed, her stepfather and mother told her the story of Emmett Till. "They weren't trying to torture me, they just wanted me to be aware."

But it wasn't just black people who turned a judgmental eye on Mississippi. Northern publications sent teams of reporters and photographers south to cover the circuslike atmosphere of the trial. It was as if the country were preparing itself for the long, intense struggle to follow and beginning to recognize that the moral high ground belonged to its long oppressed darker children.

By December 1 of that year, the Montgomery bus boycott became the locus of the next phase of this struggle. When Rosa Parks refused to give up her seat on that day, she was but one of a number of African Americans who had done so for decades. But hers was no simple act of defiance. It was part of an organized struggle for which she had been prepared as a committed activist devoted to bringing about change. Her quiet dignity inspired the nation, and support for the efforts of the boycotters came from throughout the rest of the country.

Miles Davis was acutely aware of the political and cultural changes occurring around him. Of that period, he recalled:

> Martin Luther King was leading that bus boycott down in Montgomery, Alabama; Marian Anderson became the first black person to sing at the Metropolitan Opera. Arthur Mitchell became the first black to dance with a major white dance company, the New York City Ballet. Marlon Brando and James Dean were the new movie stars and they had this rebellious young image of the "angry young man" going for them. Rebel Without a Cause was a big movie then. Black and white people were starting to get

together and in the music world. Uncle Tom images were on their way out.
All of a sudden, everybody seemed to want anger, coolness, hipness, and
real clean, mean sophistication.[2]

The period witnessed rapid change on both international
and domestic fronts. If incidents such as the Till murder and
the Montgomery bus boycott helped to rattle things nationally,
the United States also felt international pressure to address its
centuries-old race problem. As the United States vied with the
Soviet Union to gain influence in the newly emerging third
world, the federal government felt it best to try to counter images of the United States as a racist nation. For this reason, it
sought to highlight African Americans as important contributors to national culture. In tours organized by the State Department, many jazz musicians traveled throughout the world as
cultural ambassadors. Artists such as Dizzy Gillespie, Duke
Ellington, and Louis Armstrong participated. When asked
why he had never been approached by the State Department,
Miles noted that he wasn't the type of black man who would
have done it. Anger and defiance: By now these qualities were
beginning to define Davis. And if Till's image represented bru-
talized and disfigured black manhood, Davis put forth an alternative image—arrogant, confident, and beautiful.

Although this was a period of repressive anti-Communist
hysteria and a time of major battles in the struggle for black
freedom, it was also a period of great hope and possibility. The
decolonization of countries in Africa and Asia brought inspiration to those engaged in domestic battles. Syeeda recalls that

international and domestic issues were followed closely in her household, as both her mother, Naima, and John read books, newspapers, and journals that covered every stage of the black freedom movement. Speaking of her stepfather, she remembered, "He very much loved his people. I don't know if people know that, but he did. He very much loved black people, and he was concerned for us."

Davis and Coltrane were critically aware of the political environment they inhabited. And each would come to be representative of a more rebellious side of the supposedly conformist fifties. Serious, intelligent young black men: articulate, confident, refusing the antics of earlier entertainers and self-consciously affirming the complexity and unique universality of black art forms. It is in this national context that we must place the first incarnation of Miles Davis's legendary quintet. The group, including Trane, played for the first time in September 1955 in Baltimore, Maryland, a city that sat just south of the Mason-Dixon Line, but one that had an established jazz scene—after all, it is the city that produced the venerable Lady Day—and a solid African American working-class community.

Struggle and ascent: These two words embody the spirit that characterized much of black America of that time. They also define the Miles Davis Quintet, especially the two members of its front line. While Miles entered this period with a profound sense of clarity, purpose, and direction, for Trane it would be a time of difficulty: He was engaged in a struggle with his instrument as he sought to find and hone his own musical voice, a struggle to meet the demands of his new high-profile position with the hippest and most significant band of the day, a struggle to work with the notoriously uncommunicative Miles Davis. Most especially, he still struggled to free himself of a lamentable and debilitating heroin addiction.

Coltrane joined the quintet just before his twenty-ninth birthday. The band opened on Tuesday, September 27, at Club Las Vegas in Baltimore for a one-week engagement. The day after closing on October 3, Coltrane married his companion, Naima Grubbs, for whom he would write one of his most beautiful ballads, "Naima." His band mates, including Miles, were their attendants. Having lived in Philadelphia since her teens, Naima was struck by Coltrane's lack of sophistication when she first met him: "I thought John was a very nice person, but a little on the country side. He was wearing a short-sleeved shirt with no undershirt, and he wasn't wearing socks."[3] Naima was a single mother of a five-year-old, Syeeda. Their birth names were Juanita and Antonia, respectively. Upon her conversion to Islam, Naima changed her name as well as that of her daughter. One of a number of young African Americans in Philadelphia and other northern cities who converted to Islam in the late forties and early fifties, Naima was also a music enthusiast. She'd been exposed to a wide variety of music from Western classical to the blues.

Immediately following the wedding, the band left for a quick trip to Detroit. Shortly thereafter, they debuted in New York City at Birdland. The response was tepid. *Down Beat* noted, "The band as a whole is not cohesive yet." This seems to have been the commonly held viewpoint at the time. There were moments of tension between Miles and Trane, and Miles complained of the length of Trane's solos. At the Apollo, management even turned the lights out on him during one of them.[4] Throughout his early months, disappointed Davis fans compared Trane unfavorably to Sonny Rollins. By the 1950s, Sonny Rollins was already an accomplished professional who had played and recorded with the likes of Bud Powell, Fats Navarro, and Miles. He was far more precocious than Trane. His tone was more robust and developed, he was much more rhythmically fluent and varied, and his melodic invention was superior. Miles's decision to pick Trane over Sonny still seemed a mistake to most listeners.

Sonny Fortune recalls hearing a lot of talk about Trane as the new man in Miles's band:

> I saw Trane and Miles at the Showboat {a Philadelphia nightclub}. At that time, I wasn't necessarily a Coltrane fan. . . . I was more into Sonny Rollins. . . . Trane was the guy because he was from Philly and everybody was talking about {him}. But . . . I was like, I don't know. I'm not hearing it.[5]

Despite grumblings from Rollins fans, by the time the Miles Davis Quintet began a two-week engagement at New York's Cafe Bohemia, the band was beginning to find its way. Trane grew more confident and fans began to appreciate him for his original style. George Avakian, who would produce the group's Columbia recordings, caught the band while they were at Cafe

John Coltrane looks on as the Chief lays it down. Already a leader and a trendsetter in the music, the ways in which the Chief spoke and dressed inspired his fashion-conscious fans.

Bohemia and recalls, "John Coltrane was a perfect second banana. He didn't have the flash of Sonny or [Cannonball Adderley], though he ripped off a searing solo on the last set."[6]

The common practice of booking bands in one setting for a two-week period was a great boon to the development of individual bands and the music itself. It provided a kind of residency whereby musicians could work out their relationship with the material, with one another, and with audiences. Cafe Bohemia was located in Sheridan Square in Greenwich Village. Owned by Jimmy Garofalo, the club opened in the spring of 1955; bassist Oscar Pettiford was the director of music, so the bands were always hip, new, and exciting.

With this move into the Village club scene, Davis was exposed to a new audience, one made up of artists like poets Allen Ginsberg, LeRoi Jones, William Burroughs, and Jack Kerouac and show business celebrities including Frank Sinatra, Ava Gardner, Tony Bennett, Dorothy Dandridge, Lena Horne, James Dean, and Marlon Brando. Whereas previous audiences would have been made up of jazz lovers and other hipsters, this star-filled audience indicated Miles's own new status as an important figure in American popular culture. He'd already built a following there, and many were eager to hear his new saxophonist. Joyce Johnson, writer and lover of Jack Kerouac, wrote to the famous Beat author about seeing the quintet at Cafe Bohemia:

> *I went to hear Miles Davis, who is playing at the Cafe Bohemia in the Village. He's really fine—beautiful crazy lines floating on top of each other. He stood up very straight and looked stern. The place was packed, but silent as a cathedral—everybody at the bar looked sad and a little apprehensive and there was a weeping girl with a cat's face wandering back and forth looking for jazz musicians. Then—all of a sudden, a car smacked up across the street between a house and a lamppost. The people in the front seat were trapped but giggling. A man at the bar cried, "Crazy!" threw up his arms and ran out into the street, followed by everybody except Miles Davis, who kept playing. He finished and said quietly, "Thank you for the applause," and walked off. It was like a dream.*[7]

Literary critic and novelist George Stade came to New York in 1956. He and his young wife listened to jazz during their courtship and upon graduating college moved to the Village to be close to the music and become a part of the Beat scene. Stade, a tall, stately man with a flash of silver hair, recalls hanging out at Cafe Bohemia: "It was a keyhole-shaped club: The bar opened up in the back. You could sit there or for a little more you could sit at a table and eat. We sat at the bar." The Stades went often to hear Miles. "Even then he had that 'Fuck you' attitude."

Although the band traveled a great deal, it regularly spent extended periods in residence at Cafe Bohemia. Fortunately, during this time they also recorded regularly at the Hackensack studio of Bob Weinstock's Prestige Records, where the legendary Rudy Van Gelder engineered their recordings. Though Davis and Trane in fact first recorded together for Columbia, that same year because of contractual negotiations that material could not be released before the Prestige recordings. Columbia gave the band the opportunity to rehearse, do more than one take, and at times even hire arrangers like Gil Evans. None of these resources were available under Prestige. Nonetheless, because the Prestige recording sessions were spontaneous, they have the feel of a club set or a jam session and may give us a window into what it must have been like to experience the group live.

While hindsight and history tell us that the Miles Davis Quintet was the forum for the exemplary musical expression of the two now legendary horn players, in fact the band belongs as much to the rhythm section. Philly Joe Jones, Red Garland, and Paul Chambers distinguish this group from what came

Miles looks on as "Philly" Joe Jones works out at the drum kit. On the bandstand, Philly had "that thing" that Miles loved, and off the stand he would keep Miles amused—and on his toes.

before and from all of their contemporaries. Even Miles noted, "As great as Trane was sounding, Philly Joe was the fire that was making a lot of shit happen."[8]

The band benefited from Miles's utterly unique sound and conceptual organization. Although at this stage of the game Trane was not yet a full collaborator in the sense of changing the direction of the music's flow and certainly not a co-leader (he did not choose repertoire or conceptual approaches), he *was* a new voice on tenor whose unorthodoxy lent the band a fresh feel and sound. But it was the interaction among all the members of the quintet that set it apart from the other leading jazz combos of the day.

For many, the mid-fifties are remembered as the golden era of jazz. It was a time when you could hear virtually every style of jazz played by the leading voices of each genre. Not only were the two most dynamic New Orleans players, Sidney Bechet and Louis Armstrong, alive and well, the greatest big bands—the Count Basie and Duke Ellington orchestras—were in full swing. Monk had started a new band, and although Parker died in 1955, Gillespie was still playing strongly and inventively. And that's to name only the bona fide innovators, the virtual progenitors of the art form. Beneath that there was a plethora of musicians and bands that underscored the vitality and variety of the jazz scene. Even in this heady company, Miles's band of unknowns would emerge as one of the leading lights for jazz of the mid-fifties, a remarkable achievement considering the fecundity of the field at that time.

By October 1956 when the quintet recorded "Airegin," to be released on the album *Cookin'*, Duke Ellington had already made his spectacular comeback at the Newport Jazz Festival that summer, and the Clifford Brown & Max Roach Quintet was making its mark (first with Harold Land and then with Sonny Rollins, whose path consistently crossed Trane's, in the tenor sax chair). Dave Brubeck appeared on the cover of *Time* magazine, and the Modern Jazz Quartet, one of the most successful and longest-standing jazz combos in history, had evolved to its final configuration. Still, even in this rich atmosphere, the Miles Davis Quintet found something new to present to the jazz world.

It's easy to distinguish the quintet's territory from that of the more tepid stylings of both the MJQ and Brubeck's band.

Miles certainly respected Brubeck's writing and even recorded his "In Your Own Sweet Way," released on the Prestige album *Workin' with the Miles Davis Quintet*. But even at his coolest, Miles's musical aesthetic was a long way from the European-ized sounds of the Brubeck quartet. Later, in an interview by J. Lee Anderson published in *Saturday Review,*[9] when asked about Brubeck, Miles responded:

> *What do I think of Dave Brubeck? Don't ask me that! Dave's a good friend of mine, but every time I hear him I get ill. I don't like Desmond {Brubeck's "dry as a martini" saxophonist} either. Hampton Hawes spent a weekend with Brubeck and afterwards he told me, "Miles, they were playing cottage cheese and pineapple and we were playing cabbage and clabber."*

In Miles's mind, he and Brubeck were not operating on the same terrain. While the pianist was a jazz star, especially on college campuses, his aesthetic was not the blues-drenched af-fair that the Miles Davis Quintet offered. Brubeck's music was pale enough in its watering down of the blues aesthetic to be "sickening"—or, as Miles slyly signifies through Hawes's com-ment, of a different cultural background altogether. On the other hand, Miles admired John Lewis's music very much, even though, as a leader of the third stream movement, Lewis was as genuinely interested in Western art music as was Brubeck. Davis described Lewis's "Django" as one of the best composi-tions ever. A tribute to the innovative guitarist Django Rein-hardt, it is almost like a poem in its economy and poignancy. With remarkable restraint and almost no concessions to the extroverted tendencies of jazz, the slow and dirgelike "Django" sustains an intensity and pathos made all the more beautiful through restraint.

Although Miles rarely played in contexts as staid as the MJQ, his feeling for their aesthetic can be inferred from some of his collaborations with Gil Evans, such as his reading of J. J. Johnson's "Lament," for example. But the Miles Davis Quintet was definitely hotter than either of these bands would ever want to be. Even at its coolest moments, Miles's band gave the impression that it could erupt at any second. The potential energy was always manifest; even a ballad by Davis's band never strained to rid itself of its blues connotations and instead always simmered and smoldered. The nods to symphonic music inherent in Davis's work with Evans are not so much formal as they are organic. Whatever Miles's influences were from the European aesthetic, they seemed more like genuine cultural inheritances, not status-seeking borrowings. He was able to place his musical language into multiple contexts without having to find contrived devices to make the pieces fit.

Of the leading bands of the day, the one most similar to Miles's band was the Clifford Brown & Max Roach Quintet. Its music was part of the critical mass of bands whose work signaled the triumph of black musical values in the jazz world, known historically as the hard bop movement. The instrumentation of the Brown/Roach band was the same as Davis's, and both bands were co-creators of the hard bop movement. The "senior" members of each band, Davis and Roach, had both come to national attention owing to their collaborations with Bird. Brown was one of the truly outstanding trumpet players of the early 1950s, whose playing to this day remains a standard against which to measure jazz trumpet virtuosity. The young trumpeter was a phenomenal musician. He had been playing in college bands while studying mathematics and music at two different universities when he was discovered by Parker, Gillespie, and Fats Navarro, his friend and musical model. A clean-cut young man, "Brownie" was the musical opposite of Davis. His style was bright, happy, extroverted, and built upon virtuoso technique.

Along with Kenny Clarke, Roach was a primary architect of bebop drumming. He is one of the handful of genuine jazz innovators and he continued to be an important bandleaders and conceptualist until his death in 2007. In retrospect, it is not surprising that this band, which also included Harold Land on tenor sax (replaced by Sonny Rollins in 1955), Powell on piano, and George Morrow on bass, would be one of the most original and exciting of its day. In some respects, the Brown/Roach band was more accomplished than Miles's quintet. Their ensemble work over the heads of their repertoire was more elaborate than that of Miles's band (except when Davis used Evans's arrangements, as was the case with "Round Midnight"). Melodies by the Brown/Roach band were complicated by sudden shifts in feel and time, and the execution was crisp, accurate, and cleanly articulated. A good example is their 1954 version of "I Get a Kick Out of You." The arrangement features time shifts and tightly arranged ensemble passages that stretch and contort the form with precision.

At first glance, it would seem that the Davis quintet might suffer by comparison. At this time, Miles did not exhibit the kind of virtuosity Brownie routinely displayed, and Harold Land was more technically proficient than Coltrane. He was swifter and smoother, while Trane, trying for more ambitiously original lines, occasionally stumbled. The difference in polish was even more marked when Rollins joined the Brown/Roach band. While Rollins and Coltrane would leave the decade as the two dominant voices on tenor sax, at this juncture Rollins was still the more mature musician. His tone was bigger, and the lyrical content and originality of his improvisations were brilliantly conceived and compelling in execution. Rollins, though a sideman, was in no way a junior musician to Brownie. By comparison, Trane sounds at times almost as if he were muffled. In all of the recordings he made with Miles before 1957, we can hear Trane working hard, struggling to stay apace with the swift company he kept. And although Philly Joe Jones was the engine of the band, unlike Roach, he was not a musical innovator.

Unfortunately, the Brown/Roach group would not have the chance to mature because Brownie died tragically in a car accident that also killed band mate Richie Powell in 1956. Brown was not yet twenty-six. His golden sound and exuberant playing continue to inspire young musicians more than fifty years after his death.

Like the Brown/Roach configuration before Brown's death, Miles's new quintet provided a thrilling listening experience. What might be perceived by some as a more ragged ensemble approach can also be heard simply as a rawer, grittier sound. The salient difference between the two bands, however, was in the soloing. The rhythm section's playing sizzled during the solo sections in a way that made the rhythm section in the Brown/Roach band seem pedestrian by comparison. The interplay among Philly Joe, Garland, and Chambers (revered by many as one of the greatest bass players of his generation) burned intensely where other rhythm sections merely swung. Rather than being limited to the usual conversation between the soloist and the harmonic framework of the tune accompanied by the rhythm section, the improvisations in Miles's quintet included a back-and-forth interplay among the members of the rhythm section as well as with the soloist and with the tune itself.

We can hear this in the song "Airegin," recorded in the second of the two marathon sessions Miles did to complete his Prestige obligations. It would be released on *Cookin'*. This selection embodies the idea of struggle and ascent. Written by Rollins, "Airegin" is "Nigeria" spelled backward, a nod to the anticolonial struggles that were sweeping across Africa and Asia. Inspired by the newfound political independence of several African countries, jazz musicians of the 1950s and 1960s began to pay homage to Africa in the titles and music of their compositions. Africa had figured in the imaginations of jazz musicians before. Prior to Duke Ellington's more sophisticated references to and invocations of Africa, most of the jazz references to Africa inherited some of the irreverent attitudes that operated in the minstrel and vaudeville traditions of the nineteenth century. The inattention to musical and geographic facts in labeling black music and pseudoblack music as "Ethiopian airs" and the like was only slightly removed in pejorative intent from terms like "coon songs." Although black composers did not usually succumb to these practices, often their lyrics treated African themes in a similarly jocular manner. Beginning with his historic residency at the Cotton Club in the 1920s and throughout his career, Ellington insisted on the connection between Africa and jazz. With a Garvey-like insistence upon a Pan-African understanding, he also underscored the importance of the Caribbean along with Africa.

After the independence movements of various African nations, more jazz musicians pointed to Africa with pride and often with the understanding that the continent was the source of the music's greatness. Many, like Art Blakey[10] and Archie Shepp, visited Africa to study their music and/or perform with traditional musicians. Some, such as Randy Weston and Yusef Lateef, lived in Africa for years. That all of these musicians sought to visit the continent speaks volumes about the newfound importance jazz musicians placed upon Africa in the wake of decolonization. For his part, in the late 1950s Coltrane not only played Rollins's "Airegin" with the quintet, but also recorded under his own leadership several songs that evoked Africa in their musical elements and their titles, including "Dial Africa," "Oomba," "Gold Coast," "Tanganyika Strut," "Dakar," and "Bakai." Coltrane would also later pen such compositions as "Dahomey Dance," "Liberia," "Africa," and "Tunji"—the last in honor of Nigerian-born drummer Babatunde Olatunji.

The speed at which Miles's quintet's version of "Airegin" is played highlights a sense of struggle. The tempo is much faster than the original. The harmonically suspended introduction is also longer, twenty-four bars rather than the usual eight. The bass goes back and forth from C to D-flat, basically a chromatically embellished pedal point. Rather than play straight time, Philly Joe plays above and below the high hat during the vamp, a figure that is repeated indefinitely. On this recording, the splash effect of this technique complements the ambiguity hinted at by the bass part alternating between two notes. The vamp is a long-standing technique in black music, designed to facilitate dancing in every style from the ring shout to James Brown's funk recordings. Here it represents a concession to the dance tradition in a version of black music not known for dancing. The increased tempo of this selection becomes more evident once the melody starts. The rushed feeling is exacerbated by the reading that Miles and Trane give it because the offbeat countermelody comes in not only faster, but earlier. The countermelody is really a saxophone's response to the trumpet's call. The quintet adds another response from the piano immediately after Trane's entrance. The portion of the form dedicated to this is so truncated that both the saxophone and the piano enter *and* exit before the countermelody would normally have even come in. All of these entrances and exits are punctuated with Philly Joe's accompaniment, primarily on snare drum and bass drum. The drummer creates a feeling of urgency and makes the phrases sound rushed and insistent. The total feeling of ensemble parts interlocking is helped by the drum and piano making additional counter-melodies/rhythms during the first ending that would ordinarily go to the second horn. As the band returns to the top of the melody before going on to the second and final ending, they insert an interlude, which is in effect an eight-bar intro. The rhythm section does its oscillation between two notes a semitone apart while Miles plays one note (also C pedal point) and Coltrane plays whole notes. The contrast between the swinging four/four and the suspension is dramatic, yet the forward momentum is never broken. This device is employed during the solos as well and provides the setting for a delicious melismatic sweep by Miles that soars into a screech. The tempo and the harmonic suspension provide the context for a melodic content quite unlike the bebop-inspired phrasing that characterizes most of the tune and certainly all of the version that he recorded previously with Rollins. Here is a glimpse of what was to come in the later years of the band, when Miles and especially Trane took their artistry beyond the conventions of bebop.

The buoyancy and brightness of the tempo mark the move as one worthy of celebration. But the improviser must beware: Just as the reversal of colonial fortunes, symbolized in the backward spelling of the title, was achieved through concerted effort and perseverance, so too does it take an adroit soloist capable of musical somersaults and split-timed maneuvers to successfully navigate the tune. The frequent use of pedal tones adds a sense of expectancy by suspending the harmony and creating a floating feeling. Could this be the sense of hope and newness felt by all who admired the victory over the shackles of colonialism? Maybe we can read further into the inner meanings of the tune by recognizing its ultimate reliance upon the harmonic language of the colonizing culture. Starting in a minor key (as was so often the case with hard bop compositions) but ending with a clear resolution to the relative major reinscribes Western harmonic conventions, although the pedal tones and the quickly shifting tonal centers point toward a yearning for a freer approach to these same practices.

In Western music, the final cadence of each song—and indeed of each section of a song—reinforces the hierarchical thinking that is inherent in functional harmony, one of the hallmarks of diatonic music. Think of the famous ending of the first movement of Beethoven's Fifth Symphony, for instance. Certain tones, used in specific harmonic progressions, lead toward a consonant resolution in an expected and seemingly inevitable way. The introduction of a pedal point, a repeated tone over a long duration, suspends the sense of progression that is necessary for functional harmony. Constructing the pedal point as the oscillation between two notes, rather than the customary single tone, interrupts the harmonic expectations even further. Like the innovative mixture of court cases and civil disobedience that built the civil rights movement, the band's rendition of "Airegin" subverts the expectations of the prevailing tonal system without violating it in spirit.

The Miles Davis Quintet continued its interactive call and response during the solo portions of the performance as well.

Jones and Garland play a syncopated five-note rhythm (block chords on the piano and accents on the snare drum) at the beginning of the first ending. They manage to make it sound like an improvised arrangement, partly because sometimes one will play it and the other will not, and on occasion when Red Garland lays out, Jones will play a variation of the figure. Once, he also plays it in a different place in the tune, at the beginning of the form. Listening to the newly available alternate takes of recordings by the quintet gives the impression that these accompaniments through countermelodies and counter-rhythms, though obviously worked out enough to be played in perfect synchronization on occasion, were improvised. If they were predetermined, Philly Joe and Red Garland are intelligent enough to vary them slightly and to give them, somehow simultaneously, an air of expectancy and surprise. Perhaps the exhilaration that this ensemble playing provided was similar to those moments, memorialized by musicians who heard them three decades earlier, when King Oliver sang riffs into the ear of the up-and-coming Louis Armstrong, who then harmonized them perfectly on the breaks. This kind of near telepathy, found in the workings of all the truly great bands in jazz, is one of the intangibles that made the Miles Davis Quintet so exciting.

Once again, here it is important to remember the rhythm section's contributions to the band's dynamism. Chambers, Jones, and Garland provided the environment for the tales Miles and Trane told night after night on the bandstand, as well as in the studio. On November 16, 1955, about a week

William "Red" Garland, a hard-swinging soloist, played in a robust two-handed style, and could improvise rhythmically complex accompaniment figures.

after closing at Cafe Bohemia, the quintet recorded six tunes for Prestige; they would return on May 5, 1956, and October 26, 1956, to record thirty-one tunes altogether, to be released with titles suggesting the black vernacular: *Workin', Steamin', Relaxin',* and *Cookin'*.

The two marathon sessions of 1956 completed Miles's contractual obligations with Prestige, after which he and the band hit the road again, traveling to Washington, D.C., Philadelphia, and Chicago before going to California for engagements in Los Angeles and at the Blackhawk in San Francisco. When the band appeared at Jazz City on Hollywood Boulevard and Western Avenue, one listener recalled: "It felt like [Coltrane] was struggling. His phrases were short and chopped, whereas Miles was smooth and flowing, melodically. He was like an engine that was sputtering. But he would get some things off that were utterly remarkable. It came out in bursts." Roy Thompson, then a fledgling tenor saxophonist himself, saw the band several times in Chicago. He confirms that at first Coltrane seemed to have difficulty playing with the band but later "was killing."[11] More positively, writing of their appearance in Los Angeles, arranger Sy Johnson asserted: "It destroyed West Coast Jazz overnight."[12] West Coast musicians would have to return to the woodshed in order to catch up with the innovations of the Miles Davis Quintet.

On June 5, 1956, the Miles Davis Quintet featuring Davis, Coltrane, Jones, Chambers, and Garland went into the studio to record "Tadd's Delight," a bebop composition penned by Tadd Dameron. The quintet had been together for a year. "Tadd's Delight" would eventually appear on their first recording for Columbia, the now legendary 'Round About Midnight. "Round Midnight," Monk's most familiar ballad, has become a perennial favorite of musicians, not only for its brilliant composition, innovative harmony, complex form, and beautiful melody, but also for Davis's exquisite reading of that melody, Evans's provocative arrangement, and Coltrane's solo, considered his first masterpiece on record.

While the polish and perfection of "Round Midnight" are well-known, "Tadd's Delight," by virtue of its greater reliance upon the entire band and the absence of Evans's arranging, opens a window onto the real magic of this incarnation of the quintet. Although the virtuosity and intensity of the band increased over the years, on this recording we hear, in compact form, the quintessential elements that would come to characterize this band. To fully appreciate this cut, the listener must go beyond the genius of Miles Davis and the staggering virtuosity of John Coltrane to dig a band that boasted five great talents in the history of jazz. As with other legendary rhythm sections (such as Count Basie's—Basie, Walter Page, "Papa" Jo Jones, and Freddie Green—which refined and ultimately defined jazz's basic four/four swing), Garland, Jones, and Chambers set up an instantly recognizable groove, one that not only swings, but announces the rhythmic and spiritual character of the band. As Coltrane would say later, every band has its own kind of swing. The Jones/Garland/Chambers sound, with its odd mixture of polish and rawness, was as recognizable as an old friend's gait.

Philly Joe has a crisp attack with an especially adroit left hand that allows him to use his snare drum figures to converse with the music and with individual soloists in an unpredictable but compelling fashion. Of Philly Joe, Davis asserted: "He had that thing." The playing of the head (or melody) is made more exciting as his snare alternates between a call and response to the rhythmical melody and a synchronized accompaniment to it. He keeps the music hot, placing contrapuntal textures that paid homage to the dexterity and hipness of great bebop drummers like Art Blakey, Max Roach, and Kenny Clarke and also foreshadowed the drive and electric energy of drumming in later times. Roney asserts that in Miles's mind,

Philly Joe was "the baddest drummer *after* Klook, Max, and Bu." But he would evolve to become as great as they were after he learned from their styles and that of Big Sid Catlett.

Just as important (to the ensemble *and* to Miles) was that Philly Joe Jones was hip. Roney observes, "Miles thought that Philly was the hippest person ever. I played with Philly and I think that Miles was the hippest person ever, but Miles really dug Philly. He could get the most beautiful woman in the world just by talking to her. Philly was well-read, an actor, historian, spoke several languages, and could play piano. More importantly, after Miles would play a figure, Philly Joe would 'hear' the answer. Miles would say that Jones was like a brother to him and that Philly Joe had fire."[13]

Garland plays hard, swinging lines against the sparse rhythmic left-hand punctuations. His playing here places him in the lineage of the great bebop pianist Bud Powell. But Garland also has a highly developed technique of using block chords—playing chords with both hands, in sync. Miles admired the block style of piano playing in a few of the St. Louis pianists he had heard earlier in his career.[14] Moreover, Garland was able to improvise shout backgrounds in tandem with Philly Joe's left hand. This combination added a momentum and sense of urgency to the music. The depth of the almost telepathic interplay between these two musicians was rare, usually achieved between long-term associates like Charles Mingus and Dannie Richmond, Thelonious Monk and Charlie Rouse, and only a handful of others. There are many musicians whose affinity for one another's styles and ideas are deep and compelling, but not as many whose empathy is improvised in such a synchronous manner.

Although there is a tightness and arranged quality to the music, the band had few rehearsals, lending to the music's spontaneity. This was not only a consequence of their excellent musicianship, but came also from a special understanding and, better yet, an almost psychic connection that is at the core of all great rhythm sections. Jones and Garland's connectedness and synchronicity add momentum and a sense of urgency to the music.

One of the distinguished heirs to the modern bass style pioneered by Duke Ellington's precocious Jimmy Blanton, Paul Chambers was perhaps the greatest bass virtuoso of his generation. One of a handful of bass players who could swing at any tempo, he could play arco (bowed) and pizzicato (plucked) equally well and could create solos that matched the intricacy and phrasing of contemporary horn players and pianists. In addition, his taste in choosing the right note was unerring, always combining intelligent bass lines with the kind of support that makes band members joyful and confident as they create. Chambers was also one of the last generation of bass players to grow up playing without an amplifier; consequently, his sound was huge, dark, and woody. And throughout it all, his tone was rich and resonant.

Together, these three men played music that was greater than the sum of its parts—and on this recording, they create the flying carpet that Miles and Trane ride. While the rhythm section's swing would allow any competent soloist to coast and simply stay in the groove, their style and technique also supplied creative disturbances that could inspire and drive the various soloists beyond mere competence.

Miles's entrance to his solo on "Tadd's Delight" is a descending scale ending with a simple three-note motif. The motif is based upon the tonic triad of A-flat. These notes are used the way black preachers construct their sermons, when they pick structural notes that ground the performance. The similarity to gospel practices is not in sound or style, but in function. Instead of returning constantly to a particular pitch as in the black sermonic tradition, Miles uses his three-note motif in a similar fashion. The motif is borrowed from the melody, and in the space of two brief choruses it is repeated with variations and embellishments an amazing twelve times. In the tradition of the great blues artists, who also mastered the subtleties of implication, Miles toys with and worries the motif. Here he elongates, there he truncates; here he approaches it by scalar motion, there he accompanies it with rhythmic punctuation. The result is a remarkably coherent solo that swings and draws in the listener without a glib display of virtuosity. However, upon closer scrutiny, Miles's inventiveness is revealed. His solo is the standout effort on this track in no small part because of his ability to make beautiful melodies reign supreme over chord running, while taking care to include that one note that will reveal the harmonic underpinnings in greater relief. (This is perhaps something he learned from Thelonious Monk.)

In contrast with Miles's emphasis of the melody over chord

Paul Chambers was the perfect bassist for the band and a leading talent on the instrument. In addition to the dozens of recordings together and years as Miles's band mate, Chambers and Coltrane also shared a Brooklyn apartment for a while.

running, at this point in his career Coltrane was very much interested in "running the changes." He doesn't let chords go by without making explicit reference to them in his solo melody. He would later explain that when he had started playing he was enamored of Lester Young's style, but as he matured he began to dig Coleman Hawkins. In the theoretical work *The Lydian Chromatic Concept of Tonal Organization for Improvisation,* George Russell explains that Lester Young and Coleman Hawkins offer two founding but differing models of saxophone styles. Russell likens Prez to an express train and the Bean to a local train. Prez thought in the larger tonal picture, with less emphasis on the intervening details. Here, Trane, like Hawkins before him, was careful to articulate each and every harmonic change in his solos. Miles, like Prez, almost always refrained from running the changes.

Although he does not yet display the technical brilliance of his later career, Trane's individuality is already in evidence. His phrasing is firmly in the bebop tradition, with slight unexpected rhythmic flourishes. His first phrase is recognizable as one of the pet formulas of the time. Without an actual transcription that shows the rhythmic details, it is difficult to demonstrate in words just how unexpected the next phrasing is. Trane's second phrase starts on the ninth of an F-minor chord with a descending arpeggio down to the third. He then goes back up the arpeggio to the fifteenth and then descends to the eleventh, ninth root and lands on the dominant seventh. In running the changes, he never falters, never plays a wrong set of harmonies, never clashes with the form or the other players. But his sound appears muffled—especially when compared with his playing after 1957. Also, his lines are not as continuous or as supple as those by Red Garland, who also runs the changes.

It's clear to listeners that at the time of this recording Miles is far ahead of Trane in terms of conception and execution. His use of time and space is more subtle at the micro level of his individual phrases. His choruses are more organic at the macro level of the entire solo. They appear to be sculpted in such a way that he puts as much care into the entire chorus (its shape and composition) as Trane (and other "regular" good players) gave to his individual phrases or harmonic formulas.

If Miles's playing demonstrates his confidence, there is a sense of trepidation in Coltrane. Miles is in complete control: He sees the entire tune in his mind, and he manipulates the way he travels through it with ease and from the vantage point of the whole. The interruptions in Coltrane's lines are not the organic spaces of Miles's solo; instead, they seem like necessary pauses to collect himself before moving on to the next harmonic puzzle he hopes to solve. Trane's extraordinary talent and his relative lack of maturity are both in evidence here. The ii-V7-I pattern that he plays near the beginning of his solo is a classic statement that is still quoted by jazz musicians today. The ii-V7-I is the quintessential harmonic pattern in jazz, analogous to the IV-V-I progression that is the basic harmonic formula in European art music, commonly referred to as classical music. Its structure represents a defining picture of a particular key and reveals the harmonic syntax. Learning to hear and play this progression is analogous to learning to make subject and verb agree in spoken language. However, the phrase with which Coltrane ends his solo seems awkwardly placed, almost as if he ran out of time. In contrast, Miles places all the elements of his solo with ease and foresight, lending to its air of inevitability and effortlessness.

The contrast between Miles's economic lyricism and Trane's improvisational effusiveness brings to mind the front-line collaboration between Parker and a younger Davis. But this time it was Miles's turn to lead. Here, in the mid-1950s, he takes his place as perhaps the single most important jazz musician of his time. After apprenticing with Bird, the most emulated saxophonist, Miles has taken Coltrane as apprentice and would soon help to make him the only rival to Parker's legacy.

Throughout most of 1956, the band played a number of New York venues but maintained an ongoing relationship with Cafe Bohemia. Both Trane and Miles recorded with different musicians during this period as well. On Monday, September 10, the quintet went into the studio to complete recording the selections that would appear on *'Round About Midnight*. In the short period between the recording of "Tadd's Delight" and "Round Midnight," we hear evidence of Trane's tremendous growth.

The title cut benefited enormously not only from the playing of the quintet, which was superb, but also from Miles's exquisite reading of Monk's composition and the arrangement written by Evans. It gives a clear picture of the beauty that would soon take place with other Evans/Davis large-scale collaborations. Evans's arrangement gives "Round Midnight" a dark and mysterious aura that fits Miles's ballad sound. The use of the Harmon mute on this cut and the sound that he got from it would become one of the most imitated trumpet voices of the century. The Harmon mute transforms the brassy sound of the trumpet into a wispy, hollow voice. The sound of his muted trumpet on this ballad became one of Miles's signatures. Ever since "Round Midnight," trumpet players have rarely come up with another compelling approach to the sound of Harmon-muted ballad playing. In Miles's approach, the very air used to intone the instrument can be heard. The sound is full and beautiful, yet we can still hear the air in its center, making the warmth of his sound palpable. This gesture toward humanity evinces more than a hint of vulnerability and tenderness.

With its elaborate introduction and coda, the song has an epic feel. The introduction feels timeless and rubatolike, with Miles's long tones answered by subtle and softly articulated yet highly syncopated counterrhythms by the rhythm section and a sub toned counterpoint melody by Coltrane. The subdued sound is somewhat uncharacteristic of Coltrane and suggests Miles's influence upon him since "Tadd's Delight." It is also rather "writerly" in its form, which may have been Evans's influence. By "writerly," we mean a feeling of a worked-out counterpoint against which the melody could stand independently, even though its softness implies that it is actually secondary to the melody. The theme of the melody proper is one of Monk's leaping, angular, idiosyncratic renderings, but with the harmonies and sequences that highlight its beauty rather than its playful development. Rather than the usual wry humor so often found in his compositions, the listener is confronted with a deep, almost aching beauty.

The most dramatic moment of the cut, however, may be the

interlude that Evans provides between the first reading of the melody and Coltrane's solo. After Miles's slow, restrained approach to the composition, the band suddenly erupts into a loud fanfare (without, however, violating the song's ballad tempo). Miles takes off the mute and punches out the high notes, making his quintet sound like a big band doing a shout chorus. The band's up-tempo rhythms are drawn out over the ballad tempo and leave an unusually long space, filled in only by Chambers's bass. Just when all sense of sure rhythmic footing is obscured, the band blasts one final chord and then Coltrane is off to the races at the top of the form.

It is his most cogent recorded solo to date. He manages to keep the searching quality of his lines and his unorthodox sound and approach, but he weaves such memorable melodies as to never violate the mood that has been created by Miles. Rather than his usual style of running the changes, Coltrane bases his opening statements on Monk's original melody and takes his time in the development of his solo. Gone are the hurried flurries that sometimes landed awkwardly as he reached for novel sounds. Here Coltrane is relaxed and thoughtful. He slows down and manages to get it all in—odd harmonic twists, emotion-laden runs, and a tender treatment of the original theme—without ever sacrificing his originality. Here is a player of growing maturity.

The band never goes back to the melody after Coltrane's solo. Rather, Miles enters again on Harmon mute with the tag. In formal music nomenclature, the tag is known as the coda, which means "tail" in Italian. The tag is an ending attached to the end of a performance of a song. The mood is as slow and brooding as the introduction, with Coltrane's voice blending in sub tones underneath Miles. Miles's voice is dominant at the end of the tune, but Trane is no longer stumbling his way through. He is there in full effect: articulate, confident, and soulful.

When it was released in March 1957, the single "Round Midnight" became a jukebox hit in black neighborhoods. The album, *'Round About Midnight,* sold more than all of Davis's Prestige recordings combined. When he received his first check for the album, Davis was able to purchase a Mercedes 190 SL.[15] With the success of their recordings, packed club dates, and the respect of their fellow musicians, one might think the Miles Davis Quintet was on top of the world.

In many ways, it was. Even as, or perhaps because, the band was acquiring greater visibility, Davis began to quarrel with and grow tired of Trane. Although he appreciated his talent, the impatient Davis grew weary of the curious tenor player's constant questioning and conversation about music. Those who met him at the time knew that Trane was always trying to figure out musical problems. Miles complained that "[Trane] liked to ask all these motherfucking questions back then about what he should or shouldn't play. Man, fuck that shit; to me he was a professional musician and I have always wanted whoever played with me to find their own place in the music. So my silence and evil looks probably turned him off."[16] Coltrane told an interviewer, "Miles is a strange guy; he doesn't talk much and he rarely discusses music. You always have the impression that he's in a bad mood, and that what concerns others doesn't interest him or move him. . . . And if you ask him something about music, you never know how he's going to take it. You always have to listen carefully to stay in the same mood as he!"[17]

In addition, Trane didn't like to socialize in the same way Miles did. Miles and Philly Joe were ladies' men who chased women together. Miles recalled, "[Trane] was just into playing, was all the way into the music, and if a woman was standing right in front of him naked he wouldn't have even seen her. That's how much concentration he had when he played."[18] However, Philly Joe was at times unreliable. In one instance, the drummer lowered his packed bags out of a hotel window in order to escape without paying the bill. He sometimes lived with Miles and would drive Miles's second wife, Frances, crazy, although Roney recalls Miles admitting that "[Philly] would protect her from Miles when he acted a little nuts." Philly Joe would pawn his drums and hit Miles up for money to get them out of hock. Or he would show up sick, demanding money. It got so that Miles had a "Philly fund" for such emergencies. For the historic *Milestones* record date, Philly Joe showed up with just a cymbal and snare drum. They had to call around to assemble the rest of the drum kit. Eventually, Miles went to the Gretsch factory and bought his own set of drums, which he kept free from Philly's shenanigans.

Perhaps the differences between Davis and Coltrane offer some insight into the origins of the differing versions of masculinity these two icons came to represent. Davis, who embodied the 1950s black idea of coolness and hipness, was assertive and self-assured, sexy and stylish. He insisted on being treated like the star that he was. While his music was understated and suave, in his personal life he drove fast sports cars and dated glamorous women. He would hire a black lawyer, Harold Lovette, who not only proved to be an adroit businessman and adviser, but could also talk as much shit as Miles when the occasion required it. Davis wielded Lovette like a weapon against the racist practices of managers, promoters, and club owners. Miles was very proactive when it came to bringing an end to the Sambo-like projections of black artists being dictated to by white handlers. He insisted on being paid what he felt he was worth, and he helped to improve working conditions for musicians by putting an end to the hated forty-twenty system that club owners preferred. The prevailing practice was for musicians to play forty-minute sets and to take twenty-minute breaks. The sets would start twenty minutes after the hour and continue until the top of the next hour. This meant that musicians typically would have to play three or four sets every night. Not only was this tiring, it had implications for the length of tunes that could be performed and the narrative arc that could be presented during a set of music. Miles's martial stance (he once knocked out a club owner for threatening to fine him $100 for coming after the stipulated deadline, even though he was in time to perform) could have been his adaptation of his father's independence.

Coltrane's personality was very different. Like Miles, he was a man of few words and definite actions and always described as intense, intelligent, and probing. Unlike Miles, he was universally regarded as both humble and gentle. Friends described him as "country," and although his down-home earthiness included a quirky sense of humor, he was not known for sarcastic repartee. Later in his career, even when answering critics (some of whom were not only unsympathetic but hostile), Coltrane never betrayed any rancor or bitterness he might have harbored. Instead of striking out against the critics and lambasting them for their ignorance, as other misunderstood innovators like Miles Davis or Charles Mingus would have done, Coltrane took the time to explain what he was doing and even once wrote an open letter to the critics inviting them to speak with him further about his music. Conceivably, Coltrane's comparative lack of machismo, swagger, and style has its roots in being raised and nurtured primarily by women.

However, it wasn't musical differences or conflicting styles of masculinity that ultimately drove a wedge between the two of them. It was Trane's drug habit that most frustrated Davis. Syeeda explains:

> They had a good relationship. The only reason he got fired is because he was getting high. Let's face it. He knew that. He was straight up, a no-nonsense guy. He knew that that was the problem.[19]

Trane wasn't the only junkie in the band and was possibly influenced by his band mates. Miles would tell Wallace Roney that "Philly [Joe] turned Trane out. The next thing you know he was showing up late and sneaking out. He would wear the same clothes for a week and would dig in his nose and eat his snot." However, other band members also had substance problems. Philly Joe was a notorious heroin addict, Garland was addicted as well, and Paul Chambers was an alcoholic. Davis still indulged his taste for cocaine, but at the time it didn't seem to cause him problems. But when Trane began to nod off onstage or appear on the bandstand in filthy clothing that he'd been wearing for days, Miles knew it was a challenge not only to the music, but to the image he was trying to create for club owners, audiences, and recording company executives.

Miles wanted to counter growing stereotypes of jazz musicians as drug addicts incapable of behaving in a professional manner. Avakian had surrounded him with photographers, publicists, and others who would ensure his star status, and the plan was working. He was being hailed as the black male counterpart to James Dean and Marlon Brando, known as much for his sartorial splendor and his refusal to "Tom" as for his music. He couldn't afford to take the risks being presented by Trane and Philly Joe.

Davis attributed the worsening of Trane's habit to his move to Manhattan with Naima and Syeeda in June 1956. Although much of his time was spent rehearsing and performing, he and his family also took advantage of much that the city had to offer. Syeeda recalls John and Naima attending her ballet recitals at the Frederick Douglass Community Center, their trips to Coney Island, to Sunnyside Garden for wrestling matches, to the movies, and to the Village for Hungarian food.

But in New York, where the drugs were purer and more readily available, Trane continued to struggle with heroin in spite of the fullness of his family life. For a while, he tried to wean himself off the drug by replacing it with alcohol. In between sets at Cafe Bohemia, he could be found downstairs practicing and drinking wine and beer.

Despite his attempts, one night in October 1956 Trane arrived to a gig late and high. Miles slapped him and punched him in the stomach. According to one famous version of the story, Thelonious Monk, who had been visiting them backstage, told Trane and Miles, "Man, as much as you play on that saxophone, you don't have to take nothing like that; you can come and play with me anytime. And you, Miles, you shouldn't be hitting on him like that."[20] This oft told tale has many versions, some more plausible than others. According to Roney, what happened was that Miles went to scold Trane for nodding onstage, and while scolding him, Trane began to nod again. Miles hit him to wake him up, and Monk told Coltrane, "Don't let that motherfucker talk to you like that!" Miles responded that Monk should "mind [his] fucking business," at which point Monk offered Coltrane the opportunity to play with him. Whether Monk made the offer then or later, Miles had certainly had enough of Coltrane's addiction. Within days, he replaced Trane with Sonny Rollins to close out the Bohemia stay.

After returning from a brief trip to Paris, Davis tried to reconvene the quintet with Trane. But before long, all of his sidemen were nodding onstage. Miles often spoke of his love for Trane, whom he considered "sweet," "kind," and "spiritual." Nonetheless, while he found Philly Joe's drug-related antics "amusing," he felt Trane to be "pathetic." Eventually, Davis couldn't put up with Philly Joe's antics, either. By

March 1957, Davis also fired Philly Joe and replaced him with Art Taylor. Philly Joe's departure was always provisional. Roney confirms that "whenever Philly wanted the gig, Miles would take him back." According to Roney, whenever Miles wanted to try out a new drummer, he would take Jones to hear him and ask what he thought. "Philly would be like, 'Drummer? Is there a drummer up there?'" But years later when Philly heard Tony Williams, he agreed that though he was but a teenager, Williams was the real deal.

Philly Joe Jones was like a brother to Miles. Despite all the unprofessional behavior, Miles loved Philly and loved his playing. Jones would go on playing until his death, swinging and delighting audiences with his music and his band mates with his sense of humor, wide talent, and wild antics.

Trane was not so resilient, however. After Davis fired him, he went home to Philadelphia to get his act together.

INTERLUDE

During the year 1957, I experienced, by the grace of God, a spiritual awakening which was to lead me to a richer, fuller, more productive life. At that time, in gratitude, I humbly asked to be given the means and privilege to make others happy through music. I feel this has been granted through His grace. ALL PRAISE TO GOD.

—JOHN COLTRANE

THE PERIOD FOLLOWING COLTRANE'S DEPARTURE from the Miles Davis Quintet marked a phase of growth for both musicians that laid the foundation for the revolutionary musical innovations they would make individually and together during the final years of their collaboration. There was little public outcry at Trane's departure. In fact, most critics seemed to have been pleased with the switch. Throughout his time in the band, Coltrane continued to be the subject of unfavorable comparisons with Sonny Rollins. In *Down Beat* (December 12, 1956), Nat Hentoff wrote that Coltrane "lacks Sonny's compactness of impact." Another *Down Beat* reviewer, Don Gold, wrote that the Davis "group's solidarity is hampered by the angry young tenor of Coltrane. Backing himself into rhythmic corners on flurries of notes, Coltrane sounded like the personification of motion-without-progress in jazz."[1]

Sometimes the comparisons weren't necessarily because of Rollins's superior musical gifts, but because both Trane and Philly Joe were prone to ignore professional etiquette and protocols: They often were disheveled—dressed in wrinkled suits—and were late for gigs. Some critics even made a point of mentioning the good decorum of the newly configured band after their departures: "The group is neat in appearance, and on the sets caught was quite businesslike, apparently absorbed in its work."[2]

Given the group's commercial and artistic success, today's listeners might conclude that Coltrane would have done anything to continue working with Miles Davis's quintet. He had established himself as a star voice on tenor sax and benefited enormously from the publicity that attended his presence in the quintet. However, throughout his tenure with the band, the critics remained divided over his artistry; it was a split that would remain the case for the rest of his career. The opposing camps became increasingly divided over time. There were those who found his style highly original and quirky in a positive sense. There were others who continued to think that his approach was not distinctive. Still others felt he was inept and suggested that Miles's band would fare better musically with a different saxophonist. Regardless of the critics, Miles believed the two musicians that the critics lambasted most, Philly Joe and Trane, were primarily responsible for the group's success. "Trane was blowing his ass off. . . . But as great as Trane was sounding, Philly Joe was the fire that was making a lot of shit happen."[3]

Coltrane's musical maturity began with the rapid development that he enjoyed in this setting, and other musicians certainly found his voice compelling. Although he made a few sides with Gillespie, his recording career began in earnest only after he joined the quintet. Starting in 1956, he began to appear as a sideman on several albums besides those he made with Miles. Coltrane's assessment of his playing at this time was characteristically critical. Speaking with Ira Gitler in 1960 about the "sheets of sounds," Coltrane said, "Now it is not a thing of beauty, and the only way it would be justified is if it becomes that. If I can't work it through, I will drop it." He understood that he was playing with a leader whose music demanded the highest standards of readiness and that he had to improve his technique and knowledge of harmony. His tremendous work ethic and his position onstage with the "world's greatest jazz band" produced an effect that was dear to his heart: phenomenal musical growth. Despite the artistic and financial success that attended membership in the Davis quintet, and the hard work and dues that he paid in order to make it happen, he still suffered from personal demons that interfered with his readiness for this opportunity.

Coltrane's attempts to quit using drugs were accompanied by drinking vast quantities of alcohol to ease both the discomfort of withdrawal and his severe toothaches (something that could have been a death sentence for a saxophonist). Saxophonist Jackie McLean was playing opposite the Davis quintet that April 1957 and testified that Coltrane's attempt to quit his addiction was painful to watch. Although he'd started to drink to help curb withdrawal symptoms, he nonetheless came to work "in miserable shape."

Shortly after being fired, Trane, like Miles before him, returned to his family. As the story goes, he moved back into his mother's house in Philadelphia and decided that he would rid himself of his addiction to drugs and alcohol. With the help of his wife, his mother, and some of his musician friends, especially saxophonist John Glenn, Coltrane quit heroin and alcohol without medical assistance over a two-week period. He was never able to completely give up tobacco, switching from cigarettes to cigars and eventually to a meerschaum pipe. But in May 1957, John Coltrane freed himself from heroin and alcohol.

According to Coltrane biographer J. C. Thomas, Trane went cold turkey without leaving his room, requesting only water when Naima or his mother checked in on him. In Lewis Porter's biography, however, we learn that this self-imposed confinement was in effect only during the day. At night, after sweating through the painful convulsions and nightmares of narcotic and alcohol withdrawal, Coltrane worked at the Red Rooster, a Philadelphia nightspot, with McCoy Tyner. Tyner later became a key collaborator, finding innovative ways to function as a pianist in a revolutionary quartet when Coltrane became an important bandleader in his own right. Tyner, who took the name Suleiman Saud, was a devoted Muslim. Perhaps it was Tyner's quiet devotion to music and his steadfast religiosity that made it safer for Coltrane to work while going cold turkey. Perhaps playing the saxophone was the most reliable therapy for a man who first began his seemingly obsessive studying and playing of the saxophone at the time of his father's death.

The stamina and resolve necessary to work while going through narcotic withdrawal seems almost superhuman, and indeed Coltrane's account of his withdrawal involved the supernatural. While most agree that Coltrane beat his habit during the time he spent in Philadelphia, Syeeda recalls other efforts to quit the drug. She remembers days spent at her parents' apartment on 103rd Street and Amsterdam Avenue. "I remember my mother helping him back and forth because he is really sick and I am afraid. This is what I remember for days, and then he's not so sick anymore. Shortly after that things began to go well, he's working, he's practicing long hours, and things just start to change. I had to have been about seven or eight years old." As is the case with many addicts, Coltrane probably tried on several occasions to kick his habit. If Syeeda's recollections are correct, the period she describes could have taken place in 1956 or 1957.

Coltrane's belief that God was the source of his rehabilitation is one of the crucial differences between his detoxification experience and that of Miles. Trane had been living the secular life, jazz musician style, and this certainly contributed to his susceptibility to heroin addiction. But if Miles's description of Coltrane's focus is accurate, his interest in socializing and the pursuit of hedonistic pleasures were minimal. By all accounts, Coltrane was a man who lived primarily for music and when not playing spent most of his time either practicing and studying music or with his family. He did, according to all who knew him, have a voracious appetite for good food. He was not yet known for his religiosity, but he was the grandson of two AME preachers and a product of southern black middle-class upbringing.

His Christian rearing and his serious nature played a role in how he experienced this critical juncture in his life. While detoxifying his body and spirit, Coltrane says that he "saw God." The very personal and everyday access to one's deity and to sacred space and time is a hallmark of African spirituality and religious systems, and it was certainly bequeathed to black Christianity in the Americas. The ability to "see" God, perhaps an absurdity to those who insist upon empirical evidence and observable fact, was nonetheless a plausible occurrence in the world of black spirituality. When he told his mother about his experience, far from treating it as fanciful, she grew fearful for him, warning that anyone who "sees God" will soon die. Not yet thirty-one, the saxophonist would live for only ten more years.

Trane's sobriety improved his playing automatically, but his experience with God changed him and his music more than anything else. He renewed his commitment to music by dedicating his life and art to seeking and portraying the wonders of the universe in worshipful gratitude to the Creator. The spiritual dimension of this episode in Coltrane's life made his quitting drugs not just a milestone in the recovery of his personal health and professional dedication, but also a moment of religious and spiritual conversion. He would make reference to it seven years later when he recorded his magnum opus, *A Love Supreme*. Coltrane uncharacteristically took interest in the production details concerning the album cover for that particular project, choosing the cover photograph and contributing a poem. And in a letter to the listener included in the liner notes to that album and reproduced at the opening of this chapter, he relates how he dedicated his life and music to God.

The emphasis on God's grace rather than virtue perhaps reveals the degree to which Christianity provided the framework for Coltrane's spiritual understanding. Virtue implies that one earns God's favor through righteousness. Grace implies that God's favor is a gift and unearned, man's virtue is never enough to earn the goodness bestowed upon him. Trane's wide reading of the world's scriptures and his panegyric to the Creator, also included in the album cover, suggests that his spiritual sensibility is not beholden to any orthodoxy, but rather that he saw God in all things. However, Coltrane's God is personally interested in mankind and seeks the good of all. From 1957 if not before, Coltrane strived to mirror this purposefulness and benevolence in his personal life and in his music. Music and spirituality became fused for Coltrane; in one interview, rather remarkably, he stated that becoming a better person is the route to take in order to become a better musician.[4] Coltrane was already completely devoted to music, but now bearing witness to the beauty of God's creation and goodness through the medium of music became the central focus for his life. It would immediately affect the power and scope of his music.

Perhaps it was the strength acquired from confronting the challenge of narcotics addiction head-on, perhaps the absence of narcotics allowed for an even more intense focus, or perhaps it was a new sense of purpose driven by his spiritual conversion, but the recordings of Coltrane's playing from 1957 onward reveal a stronger, clearer tone, an astonishing technique, and a more authoritative delivery than before. Gone is the hesitancy that can be detected in some of his recordings with Davis from 1955 and 1956. His playing would continue to develop and change at a meteoric rate. Even after he found a mature language to present his musical ideas and when he gained the admiration of the jazz world, he would continue to change and grow, sometimes jeopardizing the gains he had made. With hindsight, it is difficult to resist the notion that God indeed used Coltrane in such a way that he could maximize his development and achievements in the short time he would have left on earth.

Always a prodigious practicer, Coltrane redoubled his efforts and could be heard playing continuously. He practiced when by himself, he practiced when friends stopped by for social visits, he practiced during his breaks on gigs. There is even a photograph of him sitting at the dinner table with his horn around his neck. While some of Coltrane's biographers mundanely conclude that he must have had an oral fixation, his own narrative (that of being on a divine mission) is more compelling, primarily because of the results he produced. From this point on, Coltrane's music took on an added urgency and beauty. His style continued to develop as he searched for the sound that would satisfy him. It was a search that was not completed at his death. Along the way, his music and even the song titles that he chose (for instance, "Spiritual," "Amen," "Dear Lord," "Meditations," "Father, Son, and the Holy Ghost," "Prayer and Affirmation," and his best-known suite, "A Love Supreme") gave testimony to the spiritual import of his musical search.

In 1957, Coltrane's recording career blossomed. Even during his drug use, Trane had become a highly sought-after band mate. He recorded at least ten albums, including two as a leader. Sometime in the spring, Coltrane signed with Prestige with a $300 advance for each album. As a new star on the label, he had no fewer than four recording sessions in this year alone. He also co-led recordings with both Paul Quinichette, a hard bop tenor saxophonist who played in the style of Hank Mobley, and Ray Draper, a young tuba player, and—probably thanks to his new recording contract with Prestige—he made several sides with the Prestige All Stars. Aside from a session with Monk for Riverside, an independent record label, he was a sideman for a host of other recordings made by such luminaries as Johnny Griffin, Mal Waldron, Sonny Clark, Oscar Pettiford, Art Blakey, and his own erstwhile band mate Red Garland.

For all of this activity, Coltrane's most significant recording as a leader for that year was made not with Prestige, but with another independent label, Blue Note Records. He had agreed to do the date before he signed with Prestige, and Blue Note Records received permission from Prestige to issue *Blue Train,*

Coltrane's second recording as a leader. On *Blue Train* he led a sextet, featuring Lee Morgan, Curtis Fuller, Kenny Drew, and his Davis quintet band mates Paul Chambers and Philly Joe Jones. J. C. Thomas suggests that the title of the album reveals Coltrane's persistent shyness, hence his unwillingness to use the spelling contained in his name, "Trane."[5] Perhaps he was simply making another of the myriad references to trains in black music of the twentieth century. Indeed, in addition to the title cut, he penned "Locomotion" specifically for *Blue Train,* surely another such reference with its fast tempo and barreling solos.

Coltrane wrote four of the five songs used on this recording, something that would never have happened on Prestige. Because the company did things for the lowest possible costs, there were several quick dates rather than one well-produced one. Also, unlike Blue Note, Prestige did not pay for rehearsals, which also reduced the number of originals and all but ensured that the originals that did manage to be recorded would be relatively simple or based upon familiar harmonies. Unlike Prestige, Blue Note paid for rehearsals, and typically their recordings featured a higher percentage of original compositions and certainly more intricate ones.

All four of Coltrane's originals have become standards in the jazz repertoire, especially the two most difficult—"Lazy Bird" and "Moment's Notice," the latter composition so named because it was added on the spot, as another song was needed to finish off the album. Ironically, of all the songs on the album,

"Moment's Notice" is perhaps the song most played by today's young jazz musicians. It utilizes a fast tempo, chromatically shifting harmonies, pedal point in the melody, and an asymmetrical form, elements that Coltrane would continue to grow in his playing and composing in later years. "Chromatic" refers to the movement by a half-step, which is the smallest interval recognized in the diatonic system. A chromatic movement is to move from one note to the very next note, up or down. When moving to chords built upon notes that are a half-step apart, the improviser encounters difficulties in making intelligible melodic statements, since very few notes will sound good over both chords. Coltrane's increased technique allowed him to play appropriate notes, since he could phrase fast enough to turn on a dime from one tonality to another. These shifting harmonies and the way he used his technique to realize them led him to be able to move in and out of tonalities at will, choosing just how dissonant or consonant he wanted to be at a given time.

Here we first encounter Coltrane's famous "sheets of sound": a tremendously fast, glissandolike way of playing. It is as if he is playing a harp instead of a saxophone (in fact, Trane had begun listening closely to harps by 1957 and would later marry the harpist/pianist/organist Alice McCleod). The sheer velocity of his notes is a breakthrough. He also subdivides the beats in a more complex manner than was common at the time. While others divided the beat evenly into two or three or four, Trane plays with groups of five or seven or nine. The effect is not only fast, but also punctuated with odd shifts in accents.

Suddenly, it is as if we had been traveling on a highway through the plains, and then we find ourselves traveling through a mountain range with no loss of speed. Here he is providing the beginning of a new vocabulary, getting away from the postbebop formulas and introducing his personalized ones in a way that rhythmically set him apart from other players. Curiously enough, this practice was already commonplace in the playing of one musician—Thelonious Monk. No doubt playing such songs as Monk's "Trinkle Tinkle" paved the way for these asymmetrical groupings.

Another good example is his performance on "Locomotion," which featured him blowing changes designed for jam session–style explorations. Gone is the hesitancy of his contributions to the earlier quintet recordings. His control of his person and his addictions translated not only into prowess as an instrumentalist, but also into increased competence as a bandleader. As the leader of this stellar group of musicians, Coltrane had to make arrangements for a three-horn front line, including Curtis Fuller on trombone and a teenage Lee Morgan on trumpet. This called for a greater degree of harmonizing than the quintet format, which often relied on unison parts between the horns. The aplomb with which the musicians, especially Morgan, played difficult, idiosyncratic pieces like Coltrane originals "Lazy Bird" and "Moment's Notice" revealed that Coltrane had prepped his musicians well for the record date. These compositions showed Coltrane's penchant for harmonic puzzles and unusual progressions.

Much of Trane's growth during this period might also be

attributed to Monk, with whom he had begun to rehearse. He had already recorded the ethereal "Monk's Mood" in a trio setting with Monk and bassist Wilbur Ware earlier in April. It is a tender rendition that treats the melody respectfully, with most of the improvisation limited to patterns based upon diminished scales during the transition between Monk's introduction and Coltrane's reading of the melody. It was indeed a minimalist reading made all the more serene with the absence of drums on the recording.

Trane was sufficiently intrigued by the master composer's music to take regular trips from Philadelphia to Monk's home in Manhattan to learn his music. The process of learning Monk's music was very different from Trane's situation with Miles. Whereas Miles could be taciturn and diffident, Monk answered Coltrane's questions about music, at times talking for hours. Monk treated Coltrane as if he were family and took him on as a special student. Typically, Coltrane arrived at Monk's house early in the morning, often before Monk was awake. Monk would get out of bed, go to the piano, and teach Coltrane his difficult music by rote, playing each section over and over until the kinks were worked out.

Like Mingus, another great composer, Monk preferred that his sidemen learn his music by ear to facilitate the proper phrasing and interpretation. But when Coltrane persisted in having problems deciphering a passage, Monk would go to his portfolios—he had all of his music written out—hand the music to Coltrane, and then leave him to learn it.

Monk wrote mostly in the standard thirty-two-bar forms

made popular by Tin Pan Alley, but always in a highly individual manner. Despite the American songbook format, Monk's compositions do not readily reveal their sources or influences. With a gift for infectious melodies and even an occasional ditty, Monk created compositions that were rhythmically abstruse and often very difficult to master. Of Monk, Coltrane said:

> *Working with Monk brought me close to a musical architect of the highest order. I felt I learned from him in every way—sensually, theoretically, technically. I would talk to Monk about musical problems, and he would show me the answer by playing them on the piano. He gave me complete freedom in my playing, and no one ever did that before.*

The two musicians took long walks around Manhattan, listened to music, and socialized with jazz patron Baroness Nica de Koenigswarter. On occasion, they spent the night at her home listening to records and talking music. The baroness, a wealthy descendant of the Rothschild family, was a significant patron and friend of a number of jazz musicians, including Charlie Parker, who died in her suite at the Stanhope Hotel on Fifth Avenue. (Monk wrote the ballad "Pannonica" for her.)

Monk was both a great musician and a great teacher. In an interview with August Blume, Trane explained how Monk's example was instructive:

> *I learned a lot with him. I learned little things, you know, I learned to watch little things. He's just a good musician, man—if you work with a*

guy who watches the finer points of things, it kind of makes you try to watch the finer points sometimes. . . . You get the little things together, and then the whole structure will stand up.[6]

Monk's novel method of practicing may have also influenced Coltrane. Monk would play one song in tempo for an hour or more. The purpose of this exercise was to ingrain the song into Monk's brain. To play something in time means to bring an exacting standard of accuracy, and this is what builds technique. The amount of concentration required to do this for a few minutes is not negligible. The amount required to do it for an hour is virtually unheard of. His "off balance" style was not haphazard. His repertory of complicated twists and turns, unexpected leaps and clusters, was all practiced meticulously and driven into his muscle memory as well as his musical imagination. When playing with Monk, Coltrane was encouraged to take long solos and to explore his ideas at length. Playing one song for so long led to a "new concept of soloing" and furthered Coltrane's harmonic knowledge. For critic Stanley Crouch, Coltrane made "the biggest breakthroughs of his entire career" while playing with Monk. According to Crouch, this period "completely revolutionized" Coltrane rhythmically. For evidence, he would have us listen to Coltrane's solo on their recording of "Trinkle, Tinkle." In his second stint with Miles Davis, Coltrane would become known for taking very long, harmonically advanced solos. This trend grew over time, his solos becoming both lengthier and more adventurous throughout the remainder of his career. And the unusual harmonies and melodies contained in Monk's music contributed to Coltrane's sense of daring while soloing. He developed the creativity and stamina to take these lengthy solos by playing on the bandstand with Monk night after night.

Monk would also "stroll"—that is, stop playing for long periods—during Coltrane's solos. According to drummer Ben Riley, Monk even got up and danced once the music was swinging sufficiently. Without the piano reinforcing the harmonies of the song, alternate chord changes could be inserted without clashing.

This technique was all the more intriguing because of the playing style of Ware, Monk's bassist. Without the piano, the bass is the harmonic anchor of the band, and Coltrane had to rely in part upon Ware's harmonic sense for the development of his solos. In an interview with Blume, he explained how Ware opened the door to harmonic exploration:

> A bass player like Wilbur Ware, he's so inventive, man, you know he doesn't always play the dominant notes. . . . Wilbur, he plays the other way sometimes. He plays things that are foreign. If you didn't know the song, you wouldn't be able to find it. Because he's superimposing things. He's playing around, and under, and over—building tension, so when he comes back to it you feel everything sets in. But usually I know the tunes— I know the changes anyway. So we manage to come out at the end together anyway.

During this period, Monk's band, including Trane, was in residence at the Five Spot in the Bowery section of New York at 5 Cooper Square—a brief but legendary residence that highlighted both Trane's and Monk's development and a new thrust in the music. Ware did not join them for this residency; Ahmed Abdul-Malik was the bassist. George Stade recalls the Five Spot audience differed from that of Cafe Bohemia in that it was more racially mixed, there were more blacks in the audience, and if at all possible, the audience may have been a bit hipper as well. They were certainly hip enough to know that something extraordinary was happening night after night.

There is a photograph of the band at the Five Spot: Monk sits at the piano, in the foreground Abdul-Malik stands with his bass, Shadow Wilson sits at his drums, and Trane stands front and center in a pose that was becoming more characteristic of him—still grounded, both feet flat on the floor, the expression on his face indicative of his intensity (still to come were bodily motions that echoed this intensity). There is something far more confident than what we have heard on the recordings with Miles up to this point as he stands center stage, with the brilliant Monk both supporting and pushing him to greater heights.

The Five Spot gig was historic for Monk's career as well, marking the end of his forced retirement from New York club dates. Previously, he had been barred for a decade from such employment after his cabaret license was revoked owing to a draconian drug law and a zeal on the part of cops to bust jazz musicians. Monk's return to performing in New York clubs was a long awaited event, and people thronged to see him. Not only did jazz aficionados line up to see the high priest, but the audience was peppered with artists, writers, celebrities, and musicians. It was as if people knew that this engagement was historic.

Until recently, this band lived only in the memories of those who heard it and as a legend to others. Their recorded output included only studio recordings and a later club date in which Trane, who had already left to go back to Miles, was actually subbing for Charlie Rouse in a band that had personnel changes in every chair but the leader's. But in January 2005, Larry Appelbaum, studio engineer and jazz specialist at the Library of Congress, discovered a performance recorded at Carnegie Hall on November 29, 1957, by the Voice of America. The recording was housed in the Voice of America archives at the Library of Congress. Monk's son, drummer T. S. Monk, co-produced and released the newly discovered recording of the Monk quartet featuring Coltrane on the Blue Note label. According to T. S. Monk, presenting this recording of his father was the most significant act of his life. The production of this compact disc was a labor of love.

The performance features a working band with almost the original lineup from the Five Spot. The band's chemistry is obvious. Every section of every piece is coordinated among the various musicians; rather than resort to simply playing the changes of the tune, each member adds nuances and inflections that highlight the details of the compositions. The joy and creativity of all the musicians are also quite evident. While the other recordings featuring Monk and Trane are excellent, this one is transcendent, and perhaps Monk's finest recording. The sound quality is superior to that of the other known tapes of the Monk quartet, and the attention to the recording techniques and the remastering are first rate. Added to the fidelity of the recording is the quality of the concert grand piano, which has Monk in a particularly playful and explorative mood. The critics uniformly gave it their highest praise, and the record-buying public has made the release a bestseller.

Ultimately, however, the music and the spirit that the band conjures are at the heart of the recording's spectacular success. The band's playing underscores the fact that the best jazz is made by working bands and not necessarily by all-star aggregations. Every member shows evidence of familiarity with the music and with the other musicians' voices.

The Five Spot gig with Monk was pivotal for Coltrane in several ways. It came at a time when he was at the crossroads of his personal and professional life. After a long and arduous climb to the big time in the jazz world, he had blown the most high-profile gig he could have. Giving up hard drugs was just the beginning of his transformation. His renewal of faith in himself was coupled with a spiritual dedication to his music. Rehearsing, learning, and performing with such an avuncular figure and musical genius as Monk seemed to bring all the pieces together for Coltrane. He was able not only to learn, but to flex his chops and stretch out musically in a way that would characterize all of his later work.

IN 1957, Miles was busy consolidating his status as an artist of major significance and as an icon of cosmopolitan black masculinity. After terminating his quintet in April, Davis entered into one of the most productive periods of his career. It is not just the quantity that engaged the irascible trumpet player, but also the diversity of that activity that provided him the opportunity for growth. From early spring to the end of the year, three momentous occurrences helped to solidify Davis's reputation as an artist and a man: He reunited with Evans to produce *Miles Ahead,* he met and married the elegant dancer Frances Taylor, and he returned to Paris, where he composed and recorded the score for Louis Malle's *Ascenseur pour l'échafaud* (*Elevator to the Gallows*). These events marked the emergence of a more mature Miles, the Miles who would become a major figure in American culture. The marriage presents a private side of a man who seemed to grow more abusive and insecure as his public star rose. Nevertheless, by the end of this period Miles Davis would be one of the most successful and well-known American musicians of the time.

Miles Ahead, recorded in four sessions between Monday, May 6, and Monday, May 27, 1957, benefited not only from the musical innovations of the Evans/Davis pairing, but also from Avakian's gift for marketing and from a number of technological innovations as well. According to John Szwed, Avakian came up with the concept of *Miles Ahead* as a "publicity ploy" to assert that Davis was ahead of the pack. He put no limitations on the musical production except that one song, titled "Miles Ahead," would be released as a single. Evans and Davis selected all the other songs, and Evans wrote the arrangements.

In some ways, the format of the recording helped to dictate the nature of the arrangements. Avakian decided to use the twelve-inch LP, until then reserved for classical music. Miles Davis and Frank Sinatra were among the first "popular" artists to record twelve-inch LPs. Prior to *Miles Ahead,* jazz artists were recorded on ten-inch LPs. Szwed notes, "It gave [Miles] a commercial edge that very few jazz musicians would ever have."[7] The twelve-inch allowed an artist to work with a theme throughout the span of the entire album, and Evans took advantage of this by using arrangements that made the individual songs seem like parts of a larger work by writing bridges between each of them.

The album was recorded in two formats, mono and stereo, the latter relatively new at the time. With the help of stereo engineers, the recording could create the illusion that different instruments are placed spatially in different places within the room. This album most definitely benefited from this separation, not only because of the size of the band, but because of the subtle colors in the orchestra and the delicate movements among the voices. Even more important to the success of the album was the overdubbing and editing possibilities for Avakian. Evans's arrangements were designed to be heard as a complete suite, ten songs that were meticulously linked together in mood and structure through interludes and introductory materials that were carefully crafted. These segments were rehearsed and recorded separately from the songs that they connected. The perfection of the recording would have been difficult, if not impossible, as a single performance. With the overdubbing techniques, Miles could lay out during solo or ensemble passages as he wished and insert his part later. This way, he would have the advantage of having heard the tapes and the opportunity to premeditate the details he wanted to include.

Miles Ahead represents a great deal of progress and increased maturity over the important *Birth of the Cool*. It is as if the ideas of the earlier recording were able to germinate over the intervening years and finally now bear fruit. Miles's ability to take his time and to make the most of his surroundings had increased since 1949. Similarly, Evans was able to orchestrate more fully and was more adept at creating the perfect foil for Miles's sound and conception. The special blend of soloist and orchestra *and* the dynamic between improvisation and composition are both further shaped by this recording. Not only does *Miles Ahead* have the advantage of eight years of growth on the parts of Davis and Evans, it also brings into sharper focus the artistic vision guiding their collaboration. Unlike the earlier sessions, there is only one arranger and only one soloist, allowing for a fuller scope and more in-depth exploration on the part of both artists. The production of this album perfectly suited Miles's and Evans's aesthetic temperaments.

However, to Miles's dismay, when the album was released, a white woman on a sailboat graced the cover. Perhaps it was an attempt to reach a broader audience, but Miles would have preferred a black woman, and he let Columbia Records executives know of his preference. Upon the second printing, a photo of Miles replaced the sailing lady, but from then on he would insist upon using black models (most of them wives or girlfriends) for the covers of his albums, thus contributing to his reputation as an assertive black man.

The album sold close to a hundred thousand copies in its first printing, making it one of the bestselling jazz albums of the day. Its success helped both Columbia and Davis. Columbia became identified with the "concept album," and Miles Davis emerged as a new kind of jazz musician in the public eye, a "serious" artist with a broad popular audience.

New York City provided the vital, energetic venue needed for an artist of Davis's stature. While he spent days in the recording studio or in his Tenth Avenue apartment working out arrangements with Evans, Miles continued to perform throughout the city in a variety of contexts. At night, he appeared with his own band at Cafe Bohemia opposite Randy Weston's trio on July 8, 1957. The band also broadcast from this club. On July 21, the quintet appeared at the Great Bay Jazz Festival in the afternoon; and the following day, Miles started a series of concerts in Central Park, Jazz Under the Stars. The Monday evening series included artists such as Billie Holiday, Erroll Garner, Lester Young, and Gerry Mulligan.

During this period of success, Davis reacquainted himself with dancer Frances Taylor, for whom he would rewrite the lovely, tender "Put Your Little Foot Right Out (Fran-Dance)" and "Pfrancing." Taylor had come to New York to appear in the Broadway musical *Mr. Wonderful* with Sammy Davis Jr. at the time. Miles had met her once before in California, when he was still addicted to heroin. She'd danced with the prestigious Katherine Dunham dancers, had been married, and was the mother of a small child. Taylor was multilingual, well-read, sophisticated, and well-traveled. Davis was smitten; when she began to appear in *West Side Story,* he caught as many of her performances as possible. In fact, he seemed to be quite proud of her success. He credited her with firing his interest in the theater. Not only did he go to her performances, the two of them attended a number of plays together. And watching Frances perform in *Porgy and Bess* at the City Center inspired him to do the *Porgy and Bess* album in the summer of 1958.

The two fell in love, and soon Taylor moved into Davis's home on Tenth Avenue. Shortly thereafter, his controlling nature began to emerge. First he insisted she stop performing. Frances, who had been named the best dancer in the cast by the company after opening night of *West Side Story,* left the stage to live with Davis. The two would marry in 1960; she was the first woman with whom he tied the knot. (Irene had been only his common-law wife.) In spite of her sacrifice, Davis continued to see other women, including the actress and future wife of Norman Mailer, Beverly Bentley. The tumultuous marriage with Frances would last until she left him in 1965 (their divorce became final in 1968). Throughout their marriage, as Davis's star rose, he became more violent and possessive of Frances, qualities that would reappear in his relationship with his last wife, actress Cicely Tyson. Roney insists that Miles's true love in life was Frances. Roney suggests that Miles's abuse should be contextualized as occurring in a time and culture when men did things like that, especially when "ladies try to step to you." He also has heard audio love letters that Miles recorded for Frances that are retained in the Davis estate. "While he was recording for Columbia, after the sessions were over he would stay in the studio and record these love letters to Frances. They were corny letters, full of mushy sentiment. He recorded some to Cicely, too." Miles was with Cicely Tyson while Wallace was hanging out with him and Roney insists that whenever Miles was around Cicely, he was a perfect gentleman and that Cicely got her way in most things, though he allows that over time things deteriorated between them.

While Coltrane underwent a spiritual transformation that led to a personal and artistic rebirth, Davis's personal demons revealed themselves in his marriage to Frances, a woman he seems to have loved as much as he was capable. This combination of darkness and romance is evident in Davis's second major musical project of this period, the sound track for Louis Malle's *Ascenseur pour l'échafaud*.

By September 1957, Davis's band had busted. After he fired Red Garland, Art Taylor quit and Sonny Rollins went on to form his own band. Two months later, Davis returned to Europe for a series of concerts produced by Marcel Romano. While in Paris, Romano and Davis's old love, Juliette Greco, introduced him to the French film director Louis Malle. (Although Davis says he resumed his relationship with Juliette Greco, others assert he was seeing Jeannette Urtreger, whom he'd met on an earlier trip.) Malle approached Davis about creating a totally improvised score for *Ascenseur pour l'échafaud*. Excited by the prospect, Davis looked at the rushes, or day's takes, for ideas that he then jotted down. The opportunity provided Davis with a new creative experience. He had long wanted to score a film. Malle wanted one that was improvised, with musicians responding to images on the screen. He asked that the musicians play against characters rather than parallel them. Working with noted American drummer Kenny Clarke and French musicians Pierre Michelot on bass, Barney Wilen on sax, and René Urtreger (brother of Jeannette) on piano, the musicians recorded the score in four days.

Ascenseur pour l'échafaud is the dark, moody tale of a married woman (Jeanne Moreau) and her lover, an intriguing former soldier (Maurice Ronet). Together they plot to murder her husband and make it look like a suicide. Shot in black and white, the film alternates between wet street scenes, shot mostly at night, and enclosed spaces such as telephone booths, car interiors, and, most important, an elevator. To simulate the atmosphere of the film, Davis or Malle chose a dark old building on the Champs-Élysées for the recording. The musicians watched short clips and then improvised around them under Miles's direction. Malle would sometimes intervene with his own ideas. The music, especially Miles's solos, is almost a character itself, ever present even though it enters the film only occasionally.

With the score, Miles reaches a new level of artistic maturity. First of all, there is his voice on the trumpet. The beautiful, brooding lines that Miles excelled at, especially on muted trumpet, are often in evidence here. What is more developed than in his previous recordings is his ability to color and shade his tones and to inflect the intonation of his open trumpet sound. Always the owner of a clear and beautifully round sound, Miles sounds especially lush here. On "Nuit sur les Champs-Élysées," a cut that is heard near the beginning and that almost amounts to the main theme for the film, Miles plays measured, plaintive long tones with blue note inflections. The excellent rhythm section repeats a simple V-I vamp in D minor, while Miles's trumpet improvises between the minor harmony and the blues. The trumpet line is the perfect match for the film as it displays both the intensity and the measured deliberateness that are called for by the film's protagonists. The ironic distance between the violence of the action and the exterior coolness of the character during the film's first murder scene is captured perfectly by the music. The same D-minor tonality and slow pulse is used. But this time Miles's achingly slow, blues-inflected trumpet lines are accompanied by a suspended harmony. The bass plays only one note, an A, the fifth of the scale/chord that represents the tonality of the song. Both the prolonged stay over one chord and the extensive use of bass pedal points would be hallmarks of Miles's next musical achievement—modal jazz.

A mode is a scale, a collection of notes arranged in stepwise motion like the scale we learn as children: *do re mi fa so la ti do*. If you start on the first note of the scale (*do*), then it's the first mode of the major scale (Ionian). If you start on the second note of the scale (*re*), then it's the second mode of the major scale (known as Dorian), and so on. Since the days of bebop, improvisers had used chords rather than scales. Since most tunes had a different chord in each measure, or even two chords in a single measure, an improviser had to be adept at connecting a lot of disparate tonal material in a short amount of time. When Miles later introduced tunes like "Milestones" and "So What" that were based upon one or two modes for the whole song rather than twenty to forty chords for a typical thirty-two-bar song, the improviser could create his or her solo differently, using a single mode for a relatively long period of time without the strictures of changing harmonies.

Although modal improvisation and composition in jazz predates Davis, his forays into it proved significant for the history of the music. There are some prior instances of Jelly Roll Morton and Charles Mingus using these devices. Most important, the arranger and composer George Russell, who is also jazz's most important theorist, devised an entire musical philosophical system around the use of modes in improvisation. He also used them in his arranging for the Dizzy Gillespie big band on the 1947 recording "Cubana Be/Cubana Bop." When Miles was playing with Bird, after having dropped out of Juilliard, he and Russell spent hours talking about these theories as Russell was developing them. And it would be the Miles Davis Sextet that would place modal jazz on the map and inspire Coltrane and others to continue to develop along those lines. The film score for *Ascenseur pour l'échafaud* is a poignant precursor to the historic modal "experiments" of *Kind of Blue* and *Milestones*.

Another felicitous moment, this time for Miles's trumpet playing rather than his composing/arranging, occurs during a scene where a young couple steals the protagonist's car for a joyride. This is one of the only happy moments in the film, and Miles's group plays a splendidly crisp and fast improvisation based upon the chords to "Sweet Georgia Brown." While no new musical ground is necessarily broken in this instance, listeners are treated to one of Davis's most extroverted solos to that date. The brisk pace is always swinging thanks to the brushwork of Clarke and the deft bass playing of Michelot. Miles abandons his usual hide-and-seek style and blows a long, energetic, tightly controlled solo that perfectly enhances the moment of infectious joy. The placement of the music, with respect to the directorial decisions, is tasteful as well. The chase scene is without music, for example, and in general Davis succeeded in Malle's desire to have the music provide a counterpoint to the plot and not simple mimesis. Davis recalled: "Louis was so nervous; I said to him, 'Louis, be cool.' . . . We set the right fucking mood for Paris."

While he recorded the film's score during the day, by night the band also played to a packed audience at Club St. Germain. This Parisian experience was a bit different from earlier trips. Davis was no longer the wide-eyed young black American awestruck by the magnificent city and taken by its willingness to accept him as a man and an artist. By now, he took that for granted. He was surrounded by a community of artists and intellectuals, and although he continued to love the City of Lights, he no longer entertained expatriate fantasies:

> *I really loved Paris, but I loved it to visit, because I didn't think the music could or would happen for me over there. If I lived in Paris, I couldn't just go and hear some great blues, or people like Monk and Trane and Duke and Satchmo every night, like I could in New York. And although there were good, classically trained musicians in Paris, they still didn't hear the music like an American musician did.*[8]

So while Miles continued to be dismayed by the racism and provinciality of the United States, he nonetheless knew that it remained the center of innovation for the kind of music he wanted to play.

Just before Christmas, he returned to New York, with a new sound of music in his head. And he knew just the musicians he needed to create it. Word was out that Monk was holding court at the Five Spot and that Trane was back on the scene. Insiders knew that this was a legendary jazz event not to be missed. The young and the old attended. There were artists in the audience such as Franz Kline and Willem de Kooning. And the musicians came, Bud Powell, J. J. Johnson, and others who were raving about it. Of course, Miles went to check them out as well:

I was proud of {Trane} for having finally kicked his habit, and he was
showing up regularly for the gig. And as much as I always loved Sonny's
playing in my band and Art Taylor's too—it still wasn't the same for me
as when I played with Trane and Philly Joe. I found myself missing
them.[9]

A few months after the band got hot, people would say to
Miles, "Have you heard Trane down at the Five Spot?" And
Miles would respond, "*I told y'all* Trane was bad." Then people would say, "Miles, have you heard Monk down at the Five
Spot?" "Listen, I first told you that Monk was bad; he was one
of my teachers." Miles started going to Monk's gig every
night, to the point of being late for his own gig. He had tried
out Tommy Flanagan, Art Taylor, and Jimmy Cobb but was
never satisfied with the band's sound. Eventually, Miles re-
hired Philly Joe on drums. He also hired Cannonball Adderley
and Sonny Rollins. This represented Miles's dream band, yet
he still was intrigued by Coltrane. He would say: "Trane was
playing! Bending down, socks falling down."

Miles wanted him back.

In an exchange that mirrored the conversation leading to
Coltrane's first stint with Miles Davis, Coltrane initially refused
Miles's offer, saying, "I'm having too much fun, and I'm learning a lot." Again Miles was reduced to pleading with Coltrane,
and he urged him to just come sit in with the band. One day,
Miles looked up while doing his gig and saw Coltrane walking
through the door with his horn. Miles quickly counted off his

Theodore "Sonny" Rollins, the "Saxophone Colossus," shares the front line alongside Miles on flugelhorn. Rollins had played with Thelonious Monk but would switch over to Davis's band after Trane was kicked out, with Trane taking his spot in Monk's group.

up-tempo song "Four." Said Miles, "Sonny Rollins unleashed it, playing all kinds of stuff. But Trane came on, full of love, not competitive. But that night he took the heavyweight championship! He sent Sonny to the Brooklyn Bridge; he has never been the same since."[10]

CLAWING AT THE LIMITS OF COOL:
THE MILES DAVIS SEXTET, 1958–1961

... But Trane clawed at the limits of cool
slandered sanity
with his tryin' to be born
raging
shit

—AMIRI BARAKA, "AM/TRAK"

THE YEARS FROM 1958 TO 1961 marked the culmination of Miles and Trane's collaboration. The sextet would be the launching pad for Coltrane's career as a bona fide bandleader and jazz giant. As historic and as great as the pre-1958 quintet was, it was the later versions of the band that produced two of Davis's most important recordings, including his bestselling album, *Kind of Blue.* This version of the Miles Davis group also proved to be one of the most influential in the history of jazz.

With this group, Davis popularized the compositional approach that came to be known as "modal jazz." And Coltrane unleashed his true musical nature, never permitting his humility to overshadow his confidence in and commitment to his vision. He had entered the original band as a junior to Miles. When he returned in 1958, not only was he free of substance abuse and the disorganization that attended it, he also came back with the workings of a new approach toward improvisation. Trane had worked out harmonic substitutions that were complex extensions of those of the beboppers. In a dream, Trane saw himself playing his three-on-one chord substitutions, and Bird told him to keep on practicing them, that they would provide the key to what he was seeking. Trane had received Bird's blessing. He took this gift and found his own devices for harmonic progressions that led to revolutions in his rhythmic approach, which in turn led to an increased technical facility necessary to pull off his runs.

Under Miles's leadership, Coltrane explored his ideas relentlessly, often in breathtaking leaps and turns. He churned out solos whose imaginative contours were often as spectacular as the astonishing velocity at which he phrased them. His solos were clearly among the most advanced in all the jazz world; and throughout his tenure with Miles and thereafter, the solos became longer and more daring. Indeed, during his absence from the quintet, Trane's musical ideas matured and became more original, complex, and sophisticated.

Upon Trane's return, Miles expanded the band's format from quintet to sextet, which set the stage for greater flexibility and range in its arrangements. After the untimely death of Clifford Brown, with Cannonball Adderley on alto sax, Miles on trumpet, and the new and improved Coltrane on tenor, Miles's band could lay claim to having the most accomplished front line since the Parker/Gillespie quintet of 1944 and 1945.

Cannonball Adderley was on a brief excursion to New York in 1956 when he first caught Miles's attention. However, he was still a high school music teacher in his native Florida at the time, and ended his foray into the New York music scene in order to honor his contract back home.

Multi-instrumentalist Howard Johnson recalls asking Cannonball why he was always concerned about the amount of money he could expect for gigs, even though he had almost instantly established himself as a major player in the big leagues. Adderley responded by saying that he could have chosen other professions, and had he done so, he still would have been successful. He saw no reason why he should suffer because music was his chosen profession.

Encouraged by his enthusiastic reception (Miles, Dizzy, and J. J. Johnson sat in with him when he played with Pettiford), he returned to New York in 1957 and began to lead his own band. Adderley was slated to join Gillespie's band, but when Miles expressed his interest, Adderley changed his mind. Cannonball believed that both Miles and Dizzy were among the few well-established bandleaders at the time. He went with Davis, however, because he felt that Miles was the better teacher. According to Adderley, he and Coltrane learned from Miles's ability to infer harmonic progressions or various progressions with as few as three notes. They called it "implied reference." Both Cannonball and Trane were instrumentalists with a lot of technique and developed styles that depended on their ability to weave long, serpentine lines. But Miles could imply all of the harmonies and melodies that the saxophonists referenced with a streamlined style that suggested the meaning and even the nuances with only a few notes.

Julian "Cannonball" Adderley listens as Miles plays through a Harmon mute. Miles stands in classic cool stance—now an iconic profile.

Cannonball was just as much a technical wizard on the saxophone as Trane. But where Coltrane's music could be dark and brooding, Adderley's soloing had the brightness and whimsy that was more characteristic of his obvious mentor,

Charlie Parker. An intelligent and capable man, Cannonball was able to communicate to his listeners in a direct manner that was at once comfortably bluesy and rhythmically challenging, allowing him to combine artistic and commercial success more than most musicians are capable of doing. He added a new element to the group's front line, which had oscillated between Miles's long silences, pregnant notes, and ethereal stretching of time and Coltrane's heady, "notey," almost aggressive assault. Adderley introduced a tinge of optimism to the mix. Importantly, it was an optimism that was displayed with a technical brilliance and imaginative flair that rescued it from sentimentality. The sweet, the bitter, and the peppery hot all coalesced on the front line, providing balance and relief. Miles had achieved a rare thing: He now led a band that was advanced without sacrificing wide appeal and accessibility.

Jazz critic and poet Amiri Baraka believed at the time that Adderley was not as true to the blues aesthetic as were Trane and Miles. He thought that Cannonball was more or less a faithful adherent to the tradition and the forms of the blues, but not the spirit of the blues, at least not in a revolutionary way. This view may have been influenced by Adderley's career subsequent to his time with Miles. Starting in 1960, Cannonball went on to lead one of the most popular jazz groups in history with a band that lay comfortably between the straight-ahead type of music that he made with Miles and the fusion movement that became popular during the 1970s. But many musicians do not necessarily agree with Baraka's assessment.

In the words of Rashied Ali, "Miles had the two greatest saxophonists in the world in his band. Trane had the tenor and close up 'Ball certainly had the alto."

The years of the sextet also saw an intensification of the civil rights struggle. The tactics and goals of the African American fight for freedom were slowly but definitively transforming into a struggle that made new strategies necessary. The methodical courtroom victories orchestrated by Charles Hamilton Houston, Thurgood Marshall, and others led to the historic 1954 *Brown v. Board of Education* victory and set the stage for blacks' greater participation in American society. The immediate white backlash, however, was almost equally impressive. Not only did the nation fail to integrate with all deliberate speed, state legislatures, school boards, and banks colluded to cheat African Americans out of the fruits of their labor. The reprisals, job dismissals, and foreclosures of activists' mortgages, the state's tolerance of white vigilantes, and the persistent problems of discrimination in employment and education all served to force blacks to consider more militant means of protest to better their condition.

At the end of 1958, the *Pittsburgh Courier* carried an article that concisely articulated the momentum of worldwide movements for racial and economic justice. Headlined 1958 WAS A MIRROR OF THE NEGRO'S FIGHT TO BE RECOGNIZED, the article, written by journalist George E. Pitts, declared:

> *The year 1958 fairly crackled with world-shaking events. Names like Little Rock and Sputnik became international symbols, and the world took*

*notice when African nations like Ghana and Guinea gained independence
in a culmination of the Black man's struggle for recognition.*

In February 1960, four students from the Agricultural and
Technical College in Greensboro, North Carolina, ignited a
new phase of the freedom struggle when they sat at the
"whites only" counter and asked to be served coffee. From this
point onward, African Americans continued to push the enve-
lope of civil disobedience. At this time, very few advocated
open rebellion against the social/economic order in a violent
manner; it was not deemed necessary. For the most part, the
comportment and strategies of the activists within the movement were ostensibly consistent with the codes of mainstream
America. No matter how uncivil or brutal the reprisals,
African Americans young and old made every effort to prove
themselves worthy of full inclusion in the fabric of American
life by keeping their protest free of tit-for-tat violence or even
verbal attacks.

By the late 1960s, the old forms of civil disobedience were
no longer satisfactory for a younger generation—a generation
that came to possess a new sense of urgency and militancy.
Like the younger activists, Coltrane would chafe at the limitations of the Davis band and repertoire, finally leaving to become a bandleader: His group would be instrumental in
upsetting the established harmonic and rhythmic paradigms
of Western music. His music would become a touchstone, inspiring generations of musicians to leave behind the status quo
of Europe's diatonic system.

Many of Coltrane's new ideas were incubated in this sextet. It is captured for all to hear in the sextet's only recording, *Milestones.* The original liner notes by writer Charles Edward Smith present the new sextet as the brainchild of Miles, whom Smith establishes as the artistic visionary of his generation.[1]

Playing on the word *milestones,* Smith recounts Miles's history beginning with his birth, his introduction to music, to Bird and Diz, 52nd Street, the movement associated with *Birth of the Cool,* his recording with Gil Evans, and his score for the Louis Malle film. He seeks to establish the historic weight that attended this recording. In addition to the career-defining tone of the liner notes, *Down Beat* featured Miles in its March 6, 1958, issue. The article coincided with the album's release and gave a retrospective look at Miles's career written largely in his own words.

The old Miles Davis Quintet had worked with originals but also relied heavily upon Tin Pan Alley tunes. By contrast, save for the traditional folk song "Billy Boy," *Milestones* consisted of songs composed only by modern jazz musicians. Two were by Davis, one was by Jackie McLean, one was by Thelonious Monk, and the remainder were coauthored by John Lewis and Dizzy Gillespie. The composers were black, and the content was drenched in the blues. Four of the six compositions are blues. Three of them, "Dr. Jackle," "Sid's Ahead," and "Straight, No Chaser," are blues in the key of F, the favored key for blues by jazz players since horns first joined the guitar to make up the front line in the 1920s. The inventiveness and freshness of Miles's arrangements and the band's playing keep the repertoire from sounding repetitive. Indeed, on first listening, most people probably find it difficult to realize that two-thirds of the fare is blues and one-half of the album is based upon blues in the same key. Notably, Bird is the only other musician who could get away with this.

In terms of aesthetic, this band is the blackest of Miles's ensembles. The music is hard-driving and gritty while also sophisticated and complex. Its character is defined as much by the drummer, Philly Joe Jones, as by any other component. "That thing" that Miles admired in Jones was in full evidence on this recording and pushed the band to new levels of intensity. Coltrane used this intensity to buoy his own furious approach to the saxophone. This experience with an unusually dynamic drummer probably left an indelible impression on him, for when he started his own band, he settled upon a drummer whose force at that time was unmatched, Elvin Jones. The other factor adding to the *Milestones* set is the musical communication between Philly Joe and Red Garland; the telepathy already evident on the quintet recordings was an integral part of the group's sound for this recording as well. Trumpeter Wallace Roney rates this recording as "one of the greatest in jazz history." When asked in an interview whether *Milestones* or *Kind of Blue* (Davis's bestselling and most critically acclaimed recording) was the better recording, he exclaimed, "The band with Red [Garland] and Philly [Joe] was the strongest band ever! It was equaled only by the band with Bird and Diz. Wynton [Kelly] and Jimmy [Cobb] didn't have the same telepathy."

The opening track, Jackie McLean's "Dr. Jackle," seems to jump out at the listener. Before getting to the solos, which are based upon the blues, the head is a rather difficult bebop line. The song is not only taken at a blistering tempo, its melody is complicated and serpentine. Studio tapes of the session reveal that it took several takes for the front line to perform the melody correctly, but the master tape has a flawless execution. Philly Joe accents the many abrupt stops and syncopated rhythms and adds to the sense of forward motion that this band created so well. Garland punctuates the pause at the beginning of the form, leaving space for the drama of the horns and drums, quietly comping to bridge statements together. We can hear how Garland, following Bud Powell and Thelonious Monk's lead, is able to use the piano as a percussive as well as harmonic and melodic instrument. The members of the band all ride over the steady, clear pulse provided by Chambers. Even though the pace is very fast, his notes ring clear and full-bodied, making it easy to hear each one. While matching the ferocity of Jones's ride cymbal, Paul Chambers manages to situate each bass note with exquisite care for both its sonic resonance and its intelligent placement within the harmonic line. With its bubbling excitement and clean execution, the performance of this song announces that this is a band to be reckoned with—a group of master musicians all at the top of their game, their sounds perfectly blended for maximum impact.

While Davis sacrificed neither his hipness nor his sense of cool on this album, this track is more urgent than all his previous fare. Building upon the energy of his band, he plays with an intensity that was only hinted at before. He has not abandoned his use of bent notes or his mastery of innuendo. And he still uses space more liberally than a less secure soloist would. But to these well-established strengths he adds an ability to sustain long flights of twisted lines with the kinds of accents that only the most virtuosic of the beboppers could pull off. With his penchant for the unusual, Miles ends his solos trading with the drums. Always avoiding the clichéd and the obvious, the band doesn't open as usual by alternating four-bar phrases. Rather, Miles takes eight bars and Philly Joe takes four. As Rashied Ali and Sonny Fortune have said, Trane had elevated the level of musicianship throughout the band. Even Miles had to step up his game to be able to hang in the front line. Ali observed, "You have to consider what Cannonball and Miles say about Trane. These guys were great, but it was Trane that set the bar. It meant even more because it was not like he never made mistakes. He had been down the wrong road and achieved in spite of it."

The song really soars when the saxophonists come in battling. They trade choruses of the blues, each playing for twelve bars. Trane and Cannonball take a total of six choruses apiece. What choruses! Each man tries to fill up his chorus with as much information as possible. If there were any doubters, they could now hear that Coltrane was clean and powerful. But amazingly, Cannonball is in his own way matching Coltrane stride for stride. Garland lays out for effect at times and improvises shout choruses behind the soloists at other times, in each case highlighting the dramatic arc of the battling saxo-phones. A shout chorus is usually the penultimate chorus of a song, in which the band plays an exuberant and rhythmically interesting melody in unison before returning to the melody for the last time. It can also be a rhythmic prodding played in unison behind a soloist. Not to be outdone by the horns, Chambers then bows a solo. After demonstrating that he can keep up and play eighth notes on the bass even at this speed, he drops into a deep blues bag—instead of the flashy bebop lines, he plays a bluesy line that is folksy and funky: the kind of utter-ance that a black audience would respond to as familiar and as "talking" especially to them. His lines are the soulful setup for a brief solo on drums before the band takes the head (the melody) out. As an opener, the track announces that on this record this band is taking no prisoners. All of the kinks, occasionally appar-ent in earlier recordings, have been ironed out, and the band is ready to make its most important statements yet.

The most historically significant track would be the title song, "Milestones." Its importance is due largely to the modal character of the composition. For each of the song's two sec-tions, only one chord is used. Instead of the eight to sixteen chords that might usually take place within each eight-bar section, each chord or scale is present for eight bars at a time. While the first section, known as "the A section," is brisk and gives the feeling of marching forward, the middle section, known as "the bridge" or "the B section," has a suspended feel-ing due to the pedal point employed by the bass. The song is structured in the eight-bar phrases that characterize much of

American popular music but differs in important ways as well. The normal AABA structure is altered slightly to AABBA.[2]

Although other musicians had occasionally utilized the modal approach, "Milestones" opened the door for widespread use of this technique in the jazz world. The only musician whose recordings would popularize modal jazz in a way comparable to Davis would be Coltrane himself, who later recorded a hit with his modal treatment of "My Favorite Things" on the album of the same name. Following Davis's lead with this and the next album, *Kind of Blue,* Coltrane would go on to build a vast body of work based in part upon this improvisational method, and his achievements in this area would cause a paradigm shift in jazz during the 1960s and on into the 1970s.

In modal jazz, the lack of harmonic cycles and their attendant feeling of progression promotes a sense of timelessness. It's not so much that time does not flow, but rather that time is not on the clock. The preoccupation with punctuality and with making deadlines symbolized by playing the "correct" changes during a harmonic progression is largely absent. On the one hand, the constant reiteration of the tones in the mode (à la Miles) lent to the timeless feel of the music. In these instances, the challenge is to be melodically inventive without the crutch (or interference) of shifting harmonies. On the other hand, the improviser could stray from the mode and return to it to provide tension in the melodic line that might otherwise be missing (à la Coltrane). The rapturous feeling in turn can facilitate the impression of spiritual introspection.

This would also prove to be the explicit aim of Coltrane's later work as a bandleader.

"Milestones" gives the impression of motion with its tight, short accents made by the horns, mostly on the beat. The melody becomes syncopated by anticipating the beat only at the very end of the phrase. Philly Joe Jones plays a rim shot on the last beat of each measure, keeping the brisk tempo lively and swinging. During the bridge, it seems that time has been stretched. This elongated sense of time is realized in part by Chambers playing a rhythmic ostinato on the bass using only a pedal tone. The horn lines become smooth and *flowing* rather than short and accented, as on the A section. They *move* through the time, but not with the synchronized wall of sound of the A section. Together the saxes set waves in motion, while the trumpet seems to surf slightly above them. The drums are the only instruments that keep a steady four/four beat in this section as the piano mirrors the saxophones, and even the drums change rhythm in such a way as to cause the phrasing of the bridge to float ever so slightly above the tempo.

Miles's solo follows the modes closely. As one of the music's supreme melodists, he was definitely up to the challenges that this presented. Without the repeating cycles and the logic of tonal resolution, many players schooled in bebop would find themselves unable to construct convincing solos over modal material. However, while here both the saxophonists used more chromatic language over the modes than did Miles, each was still adept at creating cogent lines without the aid of harmonic cadences articulated by the rhythm section. Adderley's

Miles Davis and Cannonball Adderley phrasing together. With both the bluesiness and communication of a Louis Jordan and the virtuosity and harmonic sophistication of a Charlie Parker, Cannonball added a distinct voice to the band.

lines are very similar to his usual improvisations, bluesily vir-tuosic, and pleasantly easy to follow. His sound was sweeter and more consonant than that of either of the other horn men but was firmly rescued from being maudlin or sentimental ow-ing to his blues content, the intensity of his delivery, and the fecundity of his imagination. Cannonball could stretch out his ideas over long strings of measures in the music without ever seeming to run out of new thoughts or the means to execute them. Even though his style was the most indebted to tradi-tional bebop phrasing, Cannonball fits into the modal context without making the listener feel as though the horn man is trying to force a fit between his improvisation and the rhythm section.

Coltrane's frequent use of scalar runs, perfected through his patented "sheets of sound," fits the song perfectly. Already, one can hear the seriousness of his intentions as he sculpts his lines within the spaciousness of the modal form. The setting of Miles's band, with its contrasting styles and personalities, places Coltrane in relief against the more traditional Adderley and the more laconic Miles, serving to highlight rather than diminish his effect.

As is the case with all their recordings, the rhythm section is primarily responsible for the sublimity of the music. It is significant that although the band features three legendary jazz soloists on the front line, Miles decided to include a song where none of the horn players are present, not even him. On "Billy Boy," the listener is treated in effect to the Red Garland Trio. And what a trio it is. They play a tightly arranged rhythmic rendition of the old folk song "Billy Boy," an American version of a nineteenth-century English folk song originally called "William Ladd." In the process, they transform the hoary-headed chestnut into a sprightly, hip, swinging number.

The Red Garland Trio did already exist professionally outside of the Miles Davis Sextet, and Coltrane had even recorded with Prestige billed as "John Coltrane with the Red Garland Trio" during his break from Miles. By this time, the trio was the tightest in the business, the quintessential jazz rhythm section. Their supremacy was officially recognized in January

1957, when Contemporary Records released an album led by Art Pepper simply titled *Art Pepper Meets The Rhythm Section.* Under the name "The Rhythm Section," the cover reads in parentheses "Red Garland Paul Chambers Philly Joe Jones." They represent the very height of a certain style of modern music. Their playing of "Billy Boy" is so attractive that it's clear why none of the star horn players are included.

However, as might be expected, "Billy Boy" doesn't have the progressive overtones of the jazz originals. The number is imaginatively arranged and flawlessly executed, but this rendition presents nothing radically new in the musical landscape. It is in the modal conception of the title song and the many facets of the blues that the group plays on the recording that makes *Milestones* so historic. Modal jazz, glimpsed here but developed further in the next Miles Davis Sextet with the *Kind of Blue* recording, would play a major role in Coltrane's development as a soloist and as a musical thinker. But the blues remained his forte and spiritual source of his innovations.

On Monk's "Straight, No Chaser," a blues in F taken at a moderate tempo, Cannonball and Miles play in their usual style, melodic and swinging. But Coltrane comes on like a man possessed. His lines are blisteringly fast as he double-times almost the entire solo. His playing is so fast that he is able to drop whole chords and scalar passages in a mere beat or so. That he is hearing what he plays is evident, however, as he intersperses shorter, more melodic motifs within his solo, seamlessly creating a balance between the familiar and the new, the melodic and the experimental. He connects his searching style with the emotional depth traditionally associated with the blues, pushing further and further beyond convention without losing his down-home moorings, without losing the blues. After this episode in modernistic exploration, Garland and Chambers complete the offerings with more traditional choruses. Garland's is notable for his quotation of the solo on "Now's the Time" that Miles had recorded years earlier with Charlie Parker.

Milestones does indeed have the sound of Miles Davis's success: smooth and confident, looking ahead while grounded in the tradition. The cover photo is a visual portrait of this aesthetic. It is at once elegant and understated. Miles sits on a stool, holding his horn in a relaxed manner. He is dressed casually in black slacks and an exquisitely colored (especially against the burnt ochre background) green shirt, open at the collar with the sleeves rolled up. He sits relatively unadorned. His hair is natural, no longer sporting the conked hairstyle of earlier years. (His earlier cut buddy, Philly Joe, still sported the hipster/entertainer hairstyle.)

Many years later, during his interviews for Davis's autobiography, Quincy Troupe told Miles that he and his cohorts in the civil rights movement took Miles's sense of style and deportment seriously. They modeled themselves in part on their understanding of what he stood for: his dignity and take-no-shit attitude certainly, but also for the elegance of his appearance. On this cover, he does look as if he is there to take care of business, but straightforwardly, without fanfare, and on his own terms. There is no depiction of action or animation, no pictures of sexualized female models, no smoky club atmosphere or any of the other clichés of jazz hipness. There are other photos from the session that are more typical of marketing efforts, with Miles smiling and holding his horn as an object of attention. The chosen picture avoids those conventions. Just straight-ahead Miles, ready for work. He is confident and assured of his abilities and the relevance of his message. He is prepared enough to be relaxed and to be himself. Yet in the music there is a sense of fire and turbulence well contained, perhaps bubbling underneath. The self-assurance and sense of style that emanates from the photo is enhanced by the same sense of style presented in the music.

The album was a critical and popular success. Miles had his band back, and they were taking no prisoners. Among young musicians, the front line were all deemed stars: Miles, of course, but Cannonball and Trane as well. Coltrane's advances on the blues in "Straight, No Chaser" pointed the way toward the future, and Cannonball's bluesiness and technical virtuosity were similarly hard to ignore. The promoters in the industry took note as well. If some critics thought that the saxophonists were too extroverted, over time they would point to this recording as a masterpiece, the artistic harbinger of the modal experiments of *Kind of Blue,* jazz's best-selling recording.

Miles was invited to the Newport festival, where he had won his contract to Columbia through a celebrated return three years earlier, resulting in the record *'Round About Midnight.* The *Milestones* recording made it clear that this band's material was mature enough and its performance was tight enough to warrant a live recording. The Newport concert was recorded and released on one side of an album, with Monk's performance on the other side. Miles won the *Down Beat* Critics Poll for best trumpet player. His band came in fifth place in the best combo category. Later that year, he won the *Down Beat* Readers Poll by a landslide. He soon began recording *Porgy and Bess,* another of his historic collaborations with Gil Evans. On the eve of the discovery of Ornette Coleman and other jazz revolutionaries, Davis had become the leading jazz musician in the public's eyes and ears. His music, his band, his sense of style, and the perception of his dignity and self-assurance as a black man all embodied the emerging values of the times.

Unfortunately, the sextet's future was not secure. The trouble had already reached a boiling point during the recording of *Milestones,* which would sadly be this lineup's only recording. Rather than feature the piano as a solo instrument on every tune, as was customary, Red Garland soloed only on the trio selection, "Billy Boy." Instead, the bass was featured on almost every tune, which was unusual. Red, who never considered himself junior to Miles, was angry about not being allowed to solo. Consequently, Red stormed out, and Miles had to play the piano and trumpet on "Sid's Ahead." After this, Red occasionally played with Miles both on record and in live performances, but he would never again be the regular pianist for the group. Either Wynton Kelly or Bill Evans would replace him for the remainder of this band's tenure, and they would both grace the piano chair in what is Miles's most famous, bestselling, and perhaps most influential album, *Kind of Blue,* released the following year (1959).

Kind of Blue consists of five compositions, each one a modal approach to jazz writing and playing. For much of the listening public, this album presents the jazz sextet at its most perfect. The ensemble playing and the arrangements are delicately balanced. Whereas *Milestones* had announced the fiery side of the Davis group, the side that swung hard and furious, that could rip through fast tempos with aplomb and excitement, *Kind of Blue* relied less upon the rhythmic intensity associated with "blackness" in jazz. Rather than the classical overtones found in the introduction to "So What" or the impressionistic harmonies of "Blue in Green" (both from *Kind of Blue*), cuts like Monk's blues "Straight, No Chaser" highlighted the blues tradition and the freshness of Coltrane's soloing prowess. It is not that the arrangements and soloing of the cuts on *Milestones* are less subtle than those on *Kind of Blue,* but that they are more urgent and blues based. *Kind of Blue* is more understated in its execution, but more consistently groundbreaking in its harmonic and melodic conception. The use of different modes as the characteristic sound of the various tunes—Dorian mode for "So What," Mixolydian for "All Blues," and so forth—as well as the variation in meter and tempo provide a wide variety of moods. The band has a lighter sound, which may be attributed to changes in the rhythm section. Jimmy Cobb had replaced Philly Joe Jones, and Evans had replaced Garland. One problem was the unreliability of Garland. Miles loved Red's playing and preferred him to

Wynton Kelly or Bill Evans. But Garland treated Miles as a junior and never took his admonitions and discipline seriously. In addition to his walkout during the *Milestones* session, he would routinely show up late to gigs, sometimes missing the first day of the engagement altogether. For some time, Miles still preferred Red and would rehire him whenever he could. Roney remembers Miles asking, "Why do piano players always have to go to church when they get happy?" meaning that Kelly sounded churchy, whereas Miles thought of Red as bluesy and sophisticated. One week, Miles's band played opposite Bill Evans. Evans was the intermission pianist and had spent the week listening to the band just as Miles had been listening to Evans. One night when Red didn't show, Miles asked Evans to fill in. By the time Garland showed up, it was too late: He was told that "Bill had it."

After Garland left, Cannonball became the straw boss and Miles no longer had to deal with the details of paying the band. When Philly Joe came to Adderley for money from the "Philly fund," Cannonball turned him down. He also refused to pay a draw. Finally, Philly Joe issued an ultimatum: "If I don't get $200, I'm not making the next gig." Sure enough, he did not show in Boston. Cannonball referred Jimmy Cobb, who took residence as the band's drummer. Whenever Philly was around, Miles would hire him, throughout Jimmy's years with the band, but Cobb was the steady drummer until he finally got tired of Miles's fickle behavior. Miles would tell Roney, "I fired myself from Jimmy and Wynton."

The band with Bill Evans was probably Miles's best after

Bill Evans at the piano with Miles listening. Discovered while playing between sets of the Miles Davis band, Evans brought with him vast knowledge of European art music.

the "greatest band in the world" with Red and Philly Joe. In addition to the game of show-and-tell that happened between the Chief and Trane, Evans brought with him vast knowledge of European art music. He and Miles would discuss voicings, impressionist harmonies, and various devices used by classical composers. And Miles was digging it. This atmosphere permeated the band no matter who was in the piano chair. With Gil Evans, Miles had started to explore Spanish scales during the *Sketches of Spain* project. He showed these scales to Trane, and we can hear what he did with them on "Teo," which was recorded in 1961, after he had left the band, and during the same sessions that would produce "Someday My Prince Will Come."

Evans plays piano on all the tunes on *Kind of Blue* save the swinger, "Freddie Freeloader," which featured the indefatigable swinging stylings of Kelly. Cobb and Evans give the band a much lighter sound, but they lack the telepathic interplay between Garland and Jones that made the earlier sextet so explosive. Instead, Jimmy Cobb lays a smoother ride, and Bill Evans's touch likewise made the modal organization of the tunes work in part because of his stricter adherence to a supporting position within the rhythm section. (Of Evans's contribution, Miles said it provided "a quiet fire.")

The unusual harmonies and voicings that Evans had at his disposal were most pronounced in "Blue in Green," which is widely rumored to have been penned by Evans and not by Miles. Nevertheless, this tune reveals the subdued, intimate side of Miles. The rest of the band follows suit. Even Coltrane is gentle throughout the sessions. He uses motifs in a Milesian manner. In general, he takes his time on these recordings, never breaking into the double-time passages and complex chord superimpositions for which he was becoming known.

With less spectacular playing, especially minus the eruptions that usually came from the drum chair and from Coltrane, the album's mood is more cerebral than visceral. Unlike *Milestones, Kind of Blue* offers only a slight emphasis on individual solos.

The most beautiful and delicate piece may be "Flamenco Sketches." This recording is perhaps the clearest representation of the spiritual depth of Davis and his music. In spite of his dark reputation, it brings exquisite tenderness to the fore. Here questions of virtuosity and slickness are absolutely irrelevant. The song is amazingly loose and free-flowing. There is no melody, not even a set form. Rather, there is a series of five tonalities. Each mode or chord is played for as long as the soloist wants. Chambers simply plays a pedal tone for each mode, often announcing the key change by beginning with a V-I resolution. Cobb likewise plays as simply as possible, with just one brush marking the pulse and the other "stirring the soup," circling the snare drum to provide a soft, swishing sound. Evans's voicings are simple and starkly beautiful. Together, the three rhythm section players evoke a timeless, rapturous feeling that is sustained throughout the piece. The horn players stay in the same character, rarely violating the mode, and then only as chromatic coloration, adding emphasis to the resolving note within the mode rather than taking the listener away from the tonality. With no melody, Miles simply begins by improvising with a pentatonic motif on the first mode (C major) and then the succeeding four modes. The pace is exquisitely slow, and Miles's Harmon-muted sound is squeezed into the bare minimum of notes, just enough to outline the tonality. This is a prime instance of the beauty of Davis's music. There is no evidence of the Davis who callously treated women as "bitches" and sex toys; no part of this music speaks of the Davis who could be so jealous and possessive. Here we are reminded that we all are contradictory, and despite the evil of which we are capable, we are also vulnerable. Listening to "Flamenco Sketches," one can easily understand how Miles could be so beloved by all the musicians who played with him or why the women who loved him may have tolerated his abuse and nonsense. Clearly, here is a man who had a tender, patient, loving side.

The changing of the soloists does not break the spell that the band casts during Miles's opening. Coltrane does not play his glissandolike sheets of sounds. Nor does he superimpose distant harmonies over the modes, as was his custom. He plays in as minimal a fashion as possible with respect to both note choice and speed. The same is true of Cannonball and Evans. The overall effect is unforgettable, and it may be the most spiritual statement made by this band.

Throughout *Kind of Blue,* Trane began to feel his personal way into "the music."[3] Although he had always been somewhat idiosyncratic, and at times even unorthodox in his music, at this point his vision was growing both clearer and more expansive. His sound and technical facility were growing. His artistic maturity was advancing at such a pace that often when concertgoers had a chance to hear him live, his playing was noticeably different from what it sounded like on whatever recording they may have bought. The disparity between his performances and his currently available records was especially wide since Prestige was still issuing records from the first Davis quintet, which had been made in the marathon sessions several years earlier. *Workin', Steamin', Relaxin',* and *Cookin'* were made in 1956, *before* Trane's spiritual awakening, before he quit drugs, before he studied and played with Thelonious Monk. These records did not represent his current style, but they were what Prestige had in the vaults, a cache of tapes made at one time to fulfill Miles's contract before he moved to Columbia.

According to Cobb, during this period Miles was very supportive of Trane's explorations: "Miles would just play the tunes that he'd play and let Coltrane experiment on them. He'd just sit back and listen and let him go, you know? Just sort of let him have it." Cobb actually witnessed an encounter between Miles and Trane that has by now become legendary:

> *The only thing that Miles would say to him when he first started to do it, he would say things like, being diplomatic, he would say, "Look, Trane, I want you to play twenty-seven choruses instead of twenty-eight." You know, choruses. That gives him the message. . . . And {Trane would} say, "Miles," he'd say, "I get so involved in this stuff I don't know when to cut it off." So Miles said, "Take the horn out of your mouth, take it out."*

Coltrane's stature in the industry continued to rise. In addition to *Kind of Blue,* in 1959 he released a number of other recordings, including *Bags & Trane* with Milt Jackson (Atlantic),

Cannonball Adderley Quintet in Chicago (Mercury), his own *Top Tracks* (Frequenz), *Alternate Takes* (Atlantic), *Giant Steps* (Atlantic), and *Coltrane Jazz* (Atlantic). Despite these artistic successes, a few influential critics expressed their bewilderment at his extroverted and innovative soloing style by trash-talking his music. Many *Down Beat* reviews sound like Beat Downs (some musicians' nickname for the publication), as Coltrane is on the receiving end of the kind of unsympathetic music (and cultural) criticism that would run alongside the adulation that followed him throughout the rest of his career. In Coltrane criticism there seems to be no middle of the road; one either loves or hates his music. These tendencies eventually led *Down Beat* to print two reviews of Coltrane, one pro and one con. Before that method was adopted, the review of the sextet's opening night at the Jazz Seville in Hollywood reveals that though the reviewer does not understand Coltrane's music, he does understand that Trane's horn spoke to the future: "Coltrane communicated a sense of inhibition (sometimes even frustration) with his calculated understatement and contrived dissonance. On the whole, the tenor man's contributions suggested superficially stimulating, lonely and rather pathetic self-seeking. Is this truly the dilemma of the contemporary American jazz artist? One hesitates to believe so."[4]

In spite of such assessments, Coltrane was now at a level where he could no longer contain his artistic ambitions. He could not be secondary to anyone or anything; he wanted—and needed—to leave and start a band of his own. But before he could branch out, he had to deal with his dental problems, which were making it impossible at the moment for him to play with Miles or anyone else. When he came back after a few days with new teeth, Miles was fearful that he might have made a mistake, that his sound might be ruined. But Coltrane had been dealing with the pain of rotten teeth ever since he joined the band, having ruined them thanks to his excessive eating of sweets and also probably because of his earlier heroin addiction. He seemed a man on a mission, aware of the fragility of life and needing to express himself on his own terms. This driving need came with a sense of profound urgency.

Cannonball left to form a very successful band in November 1959. He was suddenly a new star with the kind of drawing power to be a leader, and he wisely took the chance of leading his own band along with his brother Nat on cornet. Tenor saxophonist Jimmy Heath made some gigs with Miles but could not get out of his parole obligations in order to tour. The merciless drug laws and the special hazard that addiction played to this generation of jazz musicians reared up once again to alter the direction of the art form.

But the difficulty of keeping his band together was not Miles's most dramatic problem in 1959. In August, two months before he received five stars in *Down Beat* for *Kind of Blue,* he was the victim of a vicious police attack in New York. After escorting a white female friend to her taxi, Miles decided to relax a bit in front of the club Birdland between his sets. A white cop rudely commanded him to move on. A proud man who did not take any shit from anyone, especially white authority, Miles did *not* move on. He told the officer that he was working at the club.

In spite of Miles's dignified, even glamorous appearance, his accomplishments, and his undeniable right to stand in front of the establishment where he was working, the cop beat him till his head was bloody. He was just an "uppity nigger," a fancy version of the Jim Dandy stereotype that had graced the minstrel stage for a century. Immediately following the beating, Miles was arrested for assault. The threat of violence that haunted his grandfather and father had found its way to Miles in the most cosmopolitan city of the nation.

Why did Miles resist? Why did he not simply walk back into the club? He understood the psychology of racist bullies and must have surmised the possible response to his defiance. Miles often told an anecdote about racist hooligans who got Max Roach's goat while the two of them were on the road together. Miles chided Max's naïveté, citing his roots in Brooklyn as a relative handicap: To Miles's eye, Roach had not acquired the ability to employ the trickster wit he himself developed in Jim Crow–era St. Louis. It is possible that Miles stood his ground knowing that a reprisal was likely, thinking it would only add to his list of achievements. Or perhaps he thought his stature would protect him. Whatever the case, Miles remained his own man even in a perilous situation.

Newspapers in the United States and Europe ran a photograph of Miles wearing a bloodied white shirt and sports coat, alongside his wife, the elegantly dressed Frances, leaving the police precinct house. The major black newspapers splashed headlines about the incident:

MILES DAVIS BEATEN BY COPS IN FRONT OF BIRDLAND

New York Age

BEATEN OVER BLONDE?

Baltimore African American

NO REASON YET FOR SKULL CRACKING

Pittsburgh Courier

Months later, in part because of the attention the case received in both the black and the white press, the charges were dismissed. Here was a man who had marshaled the forces of one of the greatest bands in history, a successful black man well-known to mainstream white America, and he was unable to escape fully the strictures of American racism.

While Miles confronted overt racism in his dealings with the police, Trane would encounter less obvious forms. Perhaps it was a different form of racial prejudice that, at least in part, fueled some of the opposition that he faced as his musicianship and his daring grew. John Tynan of *Down Beat* wrote of a Los Angeles concert: "Slashing at the canvas of his own creation, Coltrane erupted in a fantastic onrush of surrealism and disconnected musical thought best appreciated within the dark corridors of his personal psyche. The philosophical implications of his performance, with its overtones of neurotic compulsion and contempt for an audience, belong in another area of journalistic examination." He later contrasts Kelly, citing his sense of beauty and logic, with "the anarchistic Coltrane." Tynan would go on to write increasingly caustic reviews of Coltrane, until in an uncontrolled flourish he cites "evidence" that the brains of human beings were *biologically determined* to accept the Western diatonic scale! Tynan and other critics looked on Coltrane's line of development as a kind of apostasy. Trane was not someone like Ornette Coleman or Cecil Taylor, who made their names with the new thing; he had come up through the ranks, playing with name bands and demonstrating his mastery over the techniques and forms preferred by the jazz mainstream. His refusal to stay put in the comfort of success and acceptance was a difficult but necessary choice. He was intent on continuing his search for truth through music, come what may. The acrimony that he endured came not just from critics. On his last tour with Miles, in his first concert at the Olympia in Paris, some of the audience cheered and applauded for Trane while others booed. This polarization among jazz fans would characterize his reception throughout the remainder of his career. And it continues to this day.

It wasn't only the press and members of the listening public who did not fully understand or appreciate Trane's innovative way of playing. A series of exchanges between Columbia Records executives underscores the fact that even they didn't always get him. Tom McGuiness of CBS International,[5] after judging Trane's solo "off" on one recording, returned the record to Columbia executive J. G. Weihing, who in turn wrote a memo to producer Teo Macero, explaining that McGuiness disapproved of Trane's solo and asking Macero to "enlighten" them about Trane's significance. Macero responded that though the saxophone players on the recording did not have commercial appeal, they were on the music's cutting edge. He noted Coltrane's strong influence on younger players and concluded: "My personal opinion is that he is one of the greatest saxophone players in the world today reaching new heights with this dynamic style."[6]

Macero was not alone in his estimation of Trane's significance. In yet another memo, producer Irving Townsend is prophetic in his estimation of Miles's ongoing marketability and Trane's future, noting that Miles was so successful that even his sidemen had acquired great stature and popularity such that Columbia might even consider signing them, especially Trane.[7]

One thing is for sure: By 1960, Coltrane was a leader of avant-garde musicians who would shape the future of jazz. And he knew it himself. It would be the last year that he toured with Davis. He gave Davis notice. *Down Beat* carried an announcement of Trane's pending departure. When asked if there was any acrimony between Miles and Trane once he made known his intention to leave, Jimmy Cobb asserts:

No, no. Miles loved him, man. Miles, I remember in Philadelphia, Miles went to the mike and he said . . . "Trane, you know I love him, he's going

*to leave the band. . . . He's my man and I love him a lot." I never heard
him do that to nobody else.*

Gushing praise coming from the reticent Miles. According
to saxophonist John Stubblefield, who would work with Miles
in later decades, Miles continued to adore the star saxophonist
and even kept a large portrait of Coltrane on his bedroom
wall.[8]

IN STOCKHOLM, the second stop of the sextet's last European
tour with Coltrane, Karl-Erik Lindgren interviewed Trane in
between sets. The radio interview is interesting because it
gives a glimpse into Coltrane's stature among serious jazz fans
in Europe. Trane revealed that he was trying to find a way off
the ordinary path. This new direction was not "something that
[he] heard," but rather a conscious decision to discover a new
way. The interviewer also asked which of his albums were the
saxophonist's favorites. His first response, unsurprisingly, was
Giant Steps, which had been released the previous year. It had
been the first album to feature only his originals. On this album, Coltrane presented two of his most famous and often
played compositions, the title track and "Countdown." They
contain his most significant harmonic innovation, now known
simply as "Coltrane changes," which refers to the system of su-
perimposing three tonalities in the place of one tonality, each a
major third away from the other. Coltrane also mentioned *Blue
Train* and *Soultrane.* But *Giant Steps* was the most recent and
the most innovative. Metaphorically and harmonically, Coltrane

had changed—cured from his addictions, writing his own music, and finding his own harmonic language and systems of improvising. He was no longer a student in need of a teacher—not even a leader like Miles Davis.

The teacher had also learned from his erstwhile student. Miles had started incorporating brief scalar runs that were faster and covered a greater range. Speaking of their influence on each other, Rashied Ali says:

> I think Miles and Trane were good for each other. You know, they made each other play. Because when Miles finished playing, John would get up there and he would play for a little longer . . . he played and when he finished playing Miles would come back and play some more, you know, like "Wow, I can't leave it like this." And he would play more. . . . Those guys, I think they pushed each other, really.

As ever, Coltrane was practicing nonstop. He practiced in the hotels; he practiced on the bus; he practiced at the gigs in between sets. He was eating bananas by the bagful and practicing. Miles asked him why he practiced so much and was told, "I'm trying to get it all out." So Miles asked him, "Why the bananas?" Trane replied, "Gorillas eat bananas, and they're strong as a motherfucker!" Although it seems like another example of Coltrane's quirky sense of humor, the fact is that Coltrane's stamina and focus in his practice regimen had started to achieve results that seemed superhuman.

The *Live in Stockholm* album, recorded at the Stockholm Concert Hall on March 22, 1960, tells the whole story.

Coltrane is the outstanding voice of this concert. The rhythm section of Wynton Kelly, Paul Chambers, and Jimmy Cobb has moved closer to the hard swinging prototype that Philly Joe, Red, and Paul had achieved earlier, but still without the explosiveness that the earlier rhythm section could manage. Coltrane's fiery playing more than makes up for that. As was the case in 1957, Coltrane's playing here has taken another leap. He is no longer the co-leader (with Sonny Rollins) of the hard bop tenor saxophonists. He is not really bopping at all. He has moved on to new territory. A good example is his solo on "So What," the quintessential modal tune first heard on *Kind of Blue*. In this concert, his lines are longer, with more twists and turns. And they are much, much faster. He is not concerned with voice leading or slick harmonic resolutions so much as he is interested in shapes and sounds. He has found his voice within the modal context. Although he has developed the flexibility and velocity to bebop with the best of them, with the long periods on one chord in the modal context, he can take his time. The beginnings of all his solos on this recording show this increased confidence and greater sense of pacing. These solos are the most technically adventurous of his career to date, yet the patience and sensitivity that Miles brought out of his sidemen on the *Kind of Blue* album make their presence known here as well. Coltrane begins with simple statements that preface the material to come. There is no rush to completion, no evidence of nervousness, no need to get there fast, as was often the case with his first recordings with Miles. Now we are hearing Coltrane the young master—that is, the Coltrane who has found his unique voice. His is a musical path that diverges from every major voice on the scene at the time.

The content of his phrases is full of information that chafes at the restrictions of diatonic thinking. His interest in ragas and other non-Western systems of musical organization is in evidence. His music is clearly intent on leaving this mundane plane altogether and aspires to a different level of consciousness, one that escapes the sense of time and restraint available in even the hottest of hard bop music. We can hear in Trane's playing what Amiri Baraka wonderfully describes as "clawing at the limits of cool." The rhythm section, more sprightly than the year before, is still marking four/four time in the conventional way. When Coltrane forms his own quartet, he will pick musicians who develop a new approach to playing common time. This is still a great band, one of the greatest. But this recording reveals that Coltrane is the engine moving the wheels at this point. He has outstripped the parameters within which the rest of the musicians are dealing.

In a year's time, Coltrane will reinterpret "So What" as "Impressions." In "Impressions" he will fully realize the screams and yelps, the assault upon the diatonic system, implied in the Stockholm version of "So What." As documented on a series of live recordings that have surfaced over the years, between the time of the *Kind of Blue* version and Coltrane's later rendition as "Impressions," "So What" grew much more adventurous. "So What" was genteel, especially with the impressionist flourishes that Evans used in the introduction that are reminiscent of the European art music tradition. As "Impressions," the song features shrieks and moans, hollers, a whole scale assault upon the diatonic system only implied in the earlier version of "So What." The screams punctuate sinuous lines that skate in and out of the tonality.

Coltrane would write and perform "Impressions" while head of his own band, with players who were fully committed to his direction. When Coltrane's band plays "Impressions," there will be nothing "cool" about it. And the fury that it will realize will embody and articulate that of a whole new generation of young people globally, but most especially those who take up the mantle of black freedom.

Coltrane would participate in one additional recording with Miles after leaving the band. In 1961, he recorded "Someday My Prince Will Come." He shares the tenor chair on this cut with Hank Mobley. Roney contends that Miles was not happy with Mobley and cajoled Coltrane into showing up at the studio after seeing him at the Apollo. While the piece is beautifully rendered, it does not include any of the developments that Trane was pursuing while he was a member of Miles's group, nor does it include any of the fireworks that Coltrane was showing in his own quartet. The recording definitely has the Miles Davis touch in the arrangement and especially in his rendering of the melody, but this song in its relatively conventional setting can only serve as a bookend to the great collaboration between the two giants.

By *Someday My Prince Will Come,* Trane had truly moved on to the next phase of his development as an artist and maturation as a significant leader in his own right. Miles would continue to be a major force in the music, but Trane would go on to establish his own stream, garnering his own acolytes and gaining recognition as a central cultural figure in his own right. His music would become the sound track for a growing political and spiritual consciousness that came to characterize some of the more radical sections of both the black power and the anti-war struggles of the late sixties and early seventies.

According to Yasuhiro Fujioka, during this time Coltrane used to practice with Miles Davis at the music room in Davis's house at 312 W. 77th Street in Manhattan, which suggests that there was a remarkable degree of musical back-and-forth and mutual exploration between the two even after the band split. The collaboration between Miles and Trane, a relationship that started as that of master to apprentice, would end with them as two equals, men who loved and respected each other but who both needed to move beyond the extraordinary ground they covered together. Each was a forward-looking artist and innovator who pushed the music to its most expansive possibilities. Along the way, both had become international icons who would continue to inform our understanding of jazz music, black masculinity, and artistic genius.

THE TAG:
THE LEGACIES OF MILES DAVIS AND JOHN COLTRANE

I think they epitomized what I saw that had me completely bewildered and yet attracted to it. I mean, I saw cats that . . . didn't seem to have [anything] to say. Miles didn't have anything to say. He seemed to be very disinterested. [And then] . . . they get together, and bam: Music that was connected came out of them. I couldn't understand that. I was mystified. I mean, it was just adding to my reason for even wanting to identify, wanting to be a part of this. They seemed as if they'd had enlightenment that, for me, personally, I'm still in pursuit of . . . a better understanding.

—SONNY FORTUNE

INEVITABLY, TWO SUCH ICONIC FIGURES would leave multiple legacies. Each man has come to be seen as emblematic of certain qualities: The Chief is the epitome of cool, while Trane is the earnest believer and the seeker of truth. But beyond their symbolic differences, each man created the template for two dominant jazz styles.

Miles is the first jazz star to enter the ranks of those who are consistently recognized by a single name in the way that contemporary stars, especially pop stars, are occasionally honored: Madonna, Janet, Tupac, even Wynton. Pops, Lady, Prez, Sassy, Fatha, Hawk, Duke, and Count are all honorifics. Miles's glamour and coolness are rooted primarily in his music, of course, but they are more than bolstered by his physical beauty and sartorial elegance, his complicated relationships with beautiful women, and most of all, his take-no-shit attitude. And then there is the voice, damaged and reduced to almost a coarse whisper. Miles had a sincere but obscene manner of speaking that dismissed all squares.

In the decade that saw the initial publication of *Playboy* and the emergence of the man of leisure as more than patrician, as cool and hip, Davis represents the player in arresting fashion. He was a scion of a family of well-to-do black achievers; despite his de facto second-class citizenship due to racism, he *was* to the manner born. Having been indulged all of his life by a wealthy, doting father, Miles took to the role of player quite naturally, complete with the killer wardrobe, a high income, luxury cars, and the adoration of glamorous women. What he added to this profile that the majority of the Hugh Hefners of America did not was his brilliance and artistic integrity. Black brilliance and achievement were certainly not new, but it was a new day indeed when a rich black genius could so openly and brazenly flaunt his opulent lifestyle and disdain for culturally pedestrian Middle America. He was resented for his arrogance and even beaten by cops, yet he remained unbowed and unrepentant. It was as if Jack Johnson had continued to knock out white hopefuls instead of taking the fall and joining hack minstrel shows to survive in exile from his rightful profession.

Many contemporary jazz musicians still affect either the hip posture of Miles or the ascetic, spiritual posture of Coltrane. While Miles brought new force and complexity to the hipster role, it was already a time-honored, sacrosanct style for jazz musicians from Jelly Roll Morton to the present. Coltrane is the model for the other of the two dominant jazz personas. He introduced something new, however, inspiring musicians to eschew their philandering ways to pursue music with a monastic devotion.

Coltrane's iconic status derives from a different set of cultural values. Despite being the most influential saxophonist since Parker, he was not considered a hipster: His down-home roots showed in ways that Miles's did not. Coltrane never lost the soulful musicality of his North Carolina speech patterns, and at the height of his economic success he still wore Hush Puppies with expensive suits and maintained his penchant for not wearing socks. Even though he wrote the slickest harmonies in the music of the late 1950s, shot dope, and drank heavily, after his spiritual conversion in 1957 he turned his back on the hipster lifestyle. He risked professional and critical rejection in his quest for enlightenment. Trane was the country preacher who tapped into cosmic consciousness. By virtue of his sincerity and spiritual devotion, he became a saint, a prophet of black cultural liberation.

Consider, for instance, the St. John Will-I-Am Coltrane African Orthodox Church based in San Francisco, a Christian church that uses Coltrane's music in its liturgy and views all Coltrane records from 1957 onward to be divinely inspired utterances on a par with the scriptures of the Bible. Indeed, the followers of the church take it even further—they play two hours of Coltrane's music every day over the radio, as they believe Trane's music helps to keep the earth on the correct axis.

The church's pastor, Bishop Franzo King, comes from a black Pentecostal background. His alliance with the African Orthodox Church prevented deification of Trane; consequently, he and his followers had to settle for canonization. A man with Clark Kent's self-effacing humility and superhuman musical brilliance and technique, Coltrane fit the cultural expectations of a holy man.

Coltrane's cachet as a cultural icon derives largely from the 1960s, an era when young people fashioned a new society not driven by market values. As the hopefulness of civil rights movement activists encountered white intransigence, black urban youth grew impatient and began to develop a more militant movement. At the same time, with massive discontent concerning the war in Indochina, hippies and pacifists questioned the liberal/conservative consensus over American imperialism. Coltrane's figure as a man of the people seeking purity and God was important for those seeking the courage to fight the status quo.

Despite the force with which the public has placed each musician upon a pedestal—one as a demigod to coolness, the other as a saint of spiritual enlightenment—Coltrane's and Davis's extramusical personas are complex, even contradictory, in ways that are entirely befitting their art. While Miles is the brash bad boy who takes no shit and, at his worst, the violent batterer of women, he is also known as a tender and appreciated lover, a beloved bandleader, and a master teacher. Similarly, Coltrane is not simply the true believer basking in devotion and humility; he is a prophet of destruction who heralds the

Trane taking a breath between phrases. Coltrane's legendary concentration recalls stylized African sculpture that depicted persons who see into the spirit world.

new day, the crucifier of old forms, the avenger of human suffering.

The meanings of their music are as contested as the interpretations of their personas. Musicians, scholars, critics, and the jazz community at large have debated the various parts of their oeuvres, sometimes quite bitterly. Although there may never be a consensus about exactly what their music means and what we have to learn from them as humans, there will never be a doubt that they have contributed mightily to American—indeed, global—culture and that their music deserves repeated attention. "All Blues" sounds as cool now as it did fifty years ago. "Flamenco Sketches" continues to be one of the tenderest and most spiritual musical utterances ever made by human beings. "Milestones" still glides and announces urgency and elegance at the same time, showing the supreme balancing act that African Americans have been required to perfect in the United States.

Whether honored for their more mysterious qualities or self-evident traits, both men are rightly loved for their musical genius and the record of their work. Any examination of their legacies requires attention to their music as both collaborators and individual artists and to their influence on subsequent generations of musicians and on the imaginations of artists and political activists. Such an examination insists upon considerations of their meaning in the larger culture that housed them during their extraordinary musical journey. It is important to keep the audience in view as we survey their contributions to our culture, for the extent to which the audience is with the artist is a measure of how far the artist can soar. As Coltrane said, "When the audience is with you, it's like having a fifth man [in the quartet]." So let us adopt the vantage point of the audience as we consider their legacies.

The first element is the artistic influence they bequeathed to each other. Each musician learned valuable things from the other's example, but it is perhaps easier to see how Trane learned from Miles. By the time he ends his tenure with Miles, he chafed at the bit to go his own way, and deservedly so. Listening to the manner in which he dominates the musical landscape on his last tour with the band, one finds it difficult to remember that Coltrane began his tenure as Miles's junior in stature, experience, and competence. Despite Miles's reticence in the face of questions about methodology, Coltrane credits him with being one of two master teachers who influenced him greatly (the other being Thelonious Monk). These men stand out even in heady company, considering that before he had played with either Miles or Monk, Coltrane had played under great mentors such as Johnny Hodges and Dizzy Gillespie.

One quality that Coltrane developed while with the Davis group was his ability to think in choruses while improvising. One of the great joys of listening to any of the recordings of this group is the cohesion that Davis achieved with such economy and forethought. It was as if he were able to see the entire song as a canvas upon which to imply figures, splash colors, add textures. At the beginning of their collaboration, Coltrane's solos concentrated on smaller harmonic units, the separate tonalities and progressions of the tune. He also relied much more heavily upon formulas that he had studied and practiced. This practice contrasted with Davis's more lyrical approach. Coltrane seemed by comparison to be a good draftsman rather than a great artist, drawing accurate likenesses but not always integrating all of the images into a definitive statement. In addition to the staggering advances in both technique and conception that Coltrane displays on the recordings of his last tour with the band, one can hear how he could now take his time to develop his ideas *and* place them within the context of larger time frames.

Another technique that Miles introduced to Coltrane was the modal approach to writing, as evidenced on the recordings *Milestones* and *Kind of Blue*. While Miles's first experiments with modal compositions found him sticking to the notes in the mode during his solos, from the start Coltrane saw the modal composition as freeing him from harmonic strictures in the sense that he now had greater *choice* about which way to improvise. He would alternate using tonal harmonic progressions with more strictly modal passages. Playing in a situation where he felt he could go in both directions and consistently hearing the sound of alternate chord progressions played over various modal harmonies may have led to his most famous harmonic discovery of the late 1950s. While he was still playing with Miles, Coltrane recorded his instant classic *Giant Steps*. On this as well as his other recordings, he was composing in the opposite manner of Miles. While Miles began to concentrate on a modal approach and thereby cut the number of chords in his compositions, Coltrane wanted to go in another direction, as he explained:

> *Miles's music gave me an opportunity to see both sides of the question. It was simple and direct enough to superimpose chords—to stack them up—if*

you wanted, and if you wanted to play melodically, you could. I had
mixed emotions about it. Sometimes I'd follow Miles's lead and play lyri-
cally; other times I'd say, "That's the end of it," and play the other way.

In his own compositions, Coltrane stacked chords on top of chords, most notably on "Giant Steps" and "Countdown." These stacked chords made the music sound more dissonant, as there were more notes and ideas layered over any one chord than was customary. The ear had to get used to hearing those different notes juxtaposed together. Also, the melodies had to be played much faster to incorporate them all, which led to a new rhythmic feel in jazz phrasing. In the long run, this approach opened the door to freer improvisations, based upon the harmonies, as in bebop, but with an even wider array of sounds and formulas and a greater use of dissonance. These songs rely upon Coltrane's three-tonic approach (where in any given progression he could play three tonalities equidistant from one another rather than simply play the given tonality) that he made so famous not only in "Giant Steps" and "Countdown," but in many other songs as well, including "Body and Soul," "Satellite," "26-2," and "But Not for Me." Other sources can be revealed for Coltrane's startling discovery. His time with Monk, "a musical architect of the highest order," and with the harmonically adventurous bassist Wilbur Ware ("sometimes he plays the *other* way") are prime examples. But Miles's hand can be seen in the discoveries documented in recordings Trane made as a leader while he was still performing and recording with Miles. Roney maintains that Miles taught Trane the three-tonic approach by playing tritone substitutions, as he did in "Tune Up," which was recorded earlier in 1956, before Trane worked with Monk. When it was pointed out that Bird and Dizzy Gillespie had played tritone substitutions a decade earlier, Roney explained that "Bird and Diz probably did everything before, but Bird would modulate [to another key] after playing tritones, but Miles and Trane stayed in the key." An astute observation, as Trane's three-on-one approach was designed not for modulation, but for a different way of progressing within the key.

Coltrane's discoveries were also made possible by Davis's willingness to allow him to explore his ideas and to work them out within the group. That Miles did so may seem like an obvious point to make, but it cannot really be assumed. Coltrane was long-winded and remained so pretty much throughout his career. His musical verbosity wasn't always a joy for everybody concerned. Surely Coltrane's lengthy solos sometimes tried Miles's patience; nonetheless, Miles indulged Coltrane to the very end. By 1960, Coltrane was the premier soloist of the band, on occasion improvising lengthily over tunes on which Miles would not solo at all. Roney recalls that Miles took credit for starting Coltrane down this harmonic path. Miles claimed to have taught Trane to build chords on different starting points, such as the tonic, the sharp nine, and the flat nine. Roney expands: "But with Miles the triads and seventh chords built upon the different starting points would be of different qualities. A triad here, a dominant chord or diminished chord there. He would build a major seventh chord with the ninth in the root. Things like that."

Miles gave Trane not just space but the freedom to be himself, not always a given in the music world. Not only did Trane require more time than other musicians to develop and make his statements, he strayed further from the comfort zone of many listeners and critics. Miles was the number one bandleader, a man who could hire almost anybody, so his loyalty to Coltrane and his decision not to interfere with the way he played was a bold move. History has vindicated Miles's choice, but it was not as obvious in 1955 as it is today. Where Miles was terse, concise, even slick (as in hip), Coltrane was effusive, at times wild and freewheeling. Coltrane could make simple declarative statements à la Davis, as evidenced by his marvelously understated solo on "Flamenco Sketches." But his penchant for the long, involved solos that became his signature was actually developed with the Davis and Monk groups. Coltrane would adopt Miles's laissez-faire attitude with his own band. At one point, when looking for the right personnel for his group, he decided to drop Steve Kuhn, one of the first pianists to work with the Coltrane quartet. Kuhn asked what he could do to fit in better, and Coltrane told him to stick to his guns, not to change on his account. True, he let him go, but he never instructed the permanent members of his band on how to play for him. It may well be that this later reticence was something else he picked up from the Chief.

Coltrane also took a page from the quintet's book when he formed his own band in 1961, the year he quit playing with Miles. Within this new context, he would emerge as the most studied saxophonist since Charles Parker. While his entire professional career is of interest, especially his years with Miles, Trane's most cherished statements were made with his own band, known in the jazz world as "the classic quartet." The music that Coltrane made with McCoy Tyner (piano), Jimmy Garrison (bass), and Elvin Jones (drums) would change forever the way modern jazz is played. The intensity with which they played, the new ways that they explored modal harmonies, and the looser approach to rhythmic drive were additions equal in magnitude to the innovations of the bebop generation.

Coltrane's quartet frees the rhythm section in important ways, ways that led his music to evolve far beyond the stylistic boundaries respected by the Davis quintet. This quartet introduced new sounds, rhythms, ways of swinging, forms, harmonic/melodic foundations, and more. The freshness of their ideas continued to develop more or less continuously over the four years that the quartet remained intact. Eventually, each musician virtually redefined the roles played by their instrument in the traditional jazz quartet. To a large extent, the catalyst for this was Jones's drumming. In terms of force and presence, Jones shaped the band as much as did Coltrane. The drummer had been the main catalyst for the fireworks and overall excitement in Miles's first quintet with Coltrane. Philly Joe Jones's exuberant style had pushed the band in a way that was stylistically different but functionally similar to the ways in which Elvin Jones later lit the fire for Coltrane's group. Both drummers were dominant voices in their ensembles, far exceeding the timekeeping role to which drummers were accustomed. Not even in ensembles led by great drummers, such as the Max Roach groups or Art Blakey's Jazz Messengers, did the drummer occupy such a central position sonically and structurally. In the case of Elvin Jones with the John Coltrane Quartet, the drummer's style more than just increased excitement and presence. It was the innovation of the drums, the polyrhythmic reorganization of swing, and the constant juxtaposition of duple (those based upon groups of two accents or multiples thereof) and triple meters that led this band to the place where it would herald a new way for the jazz combo to exist in the world.

Miles hired the young Tony Williams for his next band—one that would rival the Coltrane band in importance. In both bands, the drummers were de facto leaders due to the strength of their playing and the way they were able to dominate the sound of their respective bands. Their rhythmic freshness allowed the entire ensemble to innovate in terms of how each instrument could function in the jazz quartet/quintet. At the same time, these bands were very different. Miles built his band around the drumming of Williams, with his kaleidoscopic ability to shift time, tempo, meters, and accents, but Miles also used the beautifully lyrical and harmonically sophisticated compositions of Wayne Shorter. Both drummers represent the twin roots of modern jazz drumming styles. Even today, Tony Williams and Elvin Jones are the two most influential postbop jazz drummers. There have been other drum innovators since the 1960s, but Tony and Elvin bring the freshest perspective and the most precise articulation of the new vision for small-combo drumming. Tony Williams and Elvin Jones were both men of genius and would have brought innovation to the music no matter what; nevertheless, they are best loved for the music they played in the bands of Coltrane and Davis. All of this had a great effect upon Miles the trumpeter as well. It is with this band that Miles reached even higher levels of trumpet virtuosity, in terms of range and intricacy of line. Roney points out Miles's solo on Heath's "Gingerbread Boy" as a shining example of Miles's prowess on the trumpet, claiming that he plays higher and more complex relationships to the harmony than either Woody Shaw or Freddie Hubbard.

When it comes to comparing the Chief with other trumpet virtuosos, the most controversial, of course, would be Wynton Marsalis, who in addition to being a trumpet virtuoso has become the official voice of jazz in the United States. The well-known feud between Davis and Marsalis took many twists and turns, with nasty barbs thrown by each man at the other. According to Roney, Miles did not like young Marsalis at first meeting and judged him to be an "Uncle Tom," ambitious and self-interested, with a personality that would allow whites to manipulate him. With regard to Marsalis's legendary technique, Miles simply said that "everybody at Juilliard can play like that; you have to in order to get in."

Unlike Coltrane, who built a repertoire and a style around the modal compositions that he wrote for his group, Miles did not yet continue along the path of modal jazz that he had popularized earlier. Another significant difference between the two groups was the role of the piano. McCoy Tyner reminds us that the piano is also a percussion instrument and in many instances acted as the rhythmic anchor for a band in which no one else performed the traditional timekeeping responsibilities. For Davis, Herbie Hancock was able to shift harmonically and melodically to accommodate whatever direction the rest of the Davis band explored. Rather than act as rhythmic and harmonic anchor, as Tyner did with the Coltrane group, Hancock mixed it up right along with the other members and thereby contributed to a more fluid style of playing nonmodal tunes.

The second element of the Miles/Trane legacy has to do with their status as innovators. Miles once said, "You can tell the history of jazz in four words: Louis Armstrong. Charlie Parker." Of course, this is an abbreviation, yet in Miles's inimitable way, he is able to imply so much from so few words (in this context, for example, "Charlie Parker" implies Thelonious Monk, Bud Powell, Sonny Criss, and so on). Now in the first decade of the twenty-first century, a similarly short but pregnant list can be extended to eight words: "Louis Armstrong. Charles Parker. Miles Davis. John Coltrane." (Assuming Lady Day is a daughter of Pops.) Jazz now exists in a post-Coltrane, post-Davis world. Many jazz heads regard Coltrane as the music's greatest innovator and perhaps as the last possible innovator. This view is overly conservative and perhaps even pessimistic. At the very least, it is belied by the fact that Davis continued to innovate after Coltrane's death in 1967, bringing new fans and controversy in his wake.

In addition to his contemporary role as chief model for the

neo–hard bop school, Davis became the undisputed leader of jazz/rock fusion, still a fecund genre forty years after he recorded *Bitches Brew.* When he began to play with electronic keyboards and electric basses, with funky vamps instead of swinging chord changes, much of his old fan base (including critics) was horrified. It was as if, faced with the popular ascent of rock music after the so-called British invasion, jazz purists dug into their trenches. For young consumers seeking to define themselves as hip, rock eventually eclipsed jazz. In response, some critics began to write and speak of a jazz mainstream. This jazz mainstream was putatively immune from the taint of filthy lucre. The aesthetics police attacked the right and the left—free jazz was excluded just as vehemently as was jazz/rock; only the center, "mainstream," or "straight ahead" jazz was considered to be true jazz. Nevertheless, Miles gained new fans as his bands began to be featured at elite rock clubs like the Fillmore. Even though his music remained experimental, the musicians from the rock side of the fusion split related to what Miles was doing. In the 1960s, he hung out with Jimi Hendrix (introduced to him by his future wife, rock artist Betty Mabry) and hired funk bassist Michael Henderson; by the 1980s, he was hanging out with Prince and covering Cyndi Lauper tunes.

While it was bad enough that Miles abdicated the jazz mainstream throne and threw in his lot with the popular musicians, what the purists really never forgave him for was the influence that he had over generations of talented *jazz* musicians. Alumni of various Miles Davis groups led every charter jazz fusion group of national importance. A partial list includes

Herbie Hancock's Headhunters; Tony Williams's Lifetime; Chick Corea, Al Di Meola, Stanley Clarke, and Lenny White's Return to Forever; John McLaughlin's Mahavishnu Orchestra; the Joe Zawinul/Cannonball Adderley group; and Wayne Shorter and Joe Zawinul's Weather Report—basically the *Who's Who* of fusion.

If fusion eventually became associated with facile technical runs devoid of deep thought and feeling, it did not start out that way. A credible argument can be made that after promising first albums, there was a general decline in many of the recordings made by even the leading fusion ensembles. Nevertheless, existing cheek by jowl with the most cynically commercial music was truly exciting, fresh, inventive jazz. Miles's version of fusion carried elements of free jazz, funk, and swing percolated into a new groove. He inspired generations of soul jazz and rock jazz musicians who are honest in their pursuits and knowledgeable about the breadth of the traditions from which they draw. Groups like the Crusaders, Kool & the Gang, and Earth, Wind & Fire were all started by erstwhile jazz musicians and used jazz in a way that not only intrigued a generation, but led many listeners and musicians from pop music to classic, acoustic styles of jazz.

The case for viewing Coltrane as an epoch-making giant in jazz is equally compelling. Even though he was introduced to modal jazz through his association with Miles, it is the John Coltrane Quartet that established the current methodology of how to play modally. The canonical sound of modal jazz is Coltrane/Jones-inspired. John Coltrane and Elvin Jones played with a force that was sonically equal to that of the rock bands of the era. They were much like guitarists who followed Jimi Hendrix's lead with distortion and electronic feedback, creating the noise that spoke against the sentimental norms of yesterday. At a time when many wanted to break out of the system (at least rhetorically), to live according to the principles of love and not the religion of acquisition, there was a need for a paradigm shift, aesthetically. There were too many people for whom mainstream artistic statements were alienating, if not entirely false. The sense of hopefulness in the steady march toward legal equality between the races broke down in many quarters along with the faith in a nonviolent end to American racism. In a similar vein, but in entirely different domains, unquestioned patriotism and allegiance to the cultural norms of the early twentieth century were also faltering. No longer were the assumed satisfactions of the domesticated "company man" or the suburban housewife enough for some young people to idealize as the good life. They needed new experiences, new values, and new ways of representing themselves. Coltrane's spirit-filled modal jazz was a partial answer for some. His is a message that is still heard throughout the jazz world and beyond.

Coltrane did more than overblow the fundamental tones on his horn to establish a new aesthetic in music. He had fury and sound enough to portray the energy of the age but was able to do so through his mastery of his instrument, the language of his idiom, and the breadth of his artistic and human vision. Whenever contemporary musicians approach modal improvisation, it is with the drive and finesse that Trane and Elvin brought. The deeper Coltrane went into his up-tempo explorations, the more it became apparent that there was a near symbiosis between him and the drummer, one feeding off the other. This level of intensity was a new part of the sonic vocabulary of jazz, marking a change in the emotional range of the public sphere. Jones and Coltrane added to this emotional intensity a formidable intellectual depth that drew listeners in with a searching spirit. It was a music that required great stamina just to listen to and follow it. Those who hung in there for the ride were rewarded in the first instance with the process of thinking and feeling that deeply. Liking or even understanding the music was always a beautiful bonus that, as with all spiritual blessings, could arrive in waves, in spurts and starts, or all at once. This approach to music making attracted disciples from several later generations, including saxophonists Billy Harper, Gary Bartz, Gary Thomas, and the late, great Arthur Rhames. Remarkably, Trane also influenced some of his peers and even his elders. Among saxophonists alone, Yusef Lateef, Rahsaan Roland Kirk, and Dexter Gordon come to mind.

The energy school also owes its day in the sun largely to Coltrane's patronage and leadership. Coltrane's group could sustain high-energy songs for as much as an hour or more, in a time when most tunes lasted only a few minutes. As Association for the Advancement of Creative Musicians saxophonist Roscoe Mitchell has said, it was a revelation to many that anyone could have such physical stamina to play forty-minute solos. It was (and remains) even more startling that Trane had the imagination and mental power to create viable ideas in that framework. Many young musicians heard this aspect of Coltrane's message and started their conception with that level of energy as already available. The first wave of energy acolytes influenced by Trane would include people like Albert Ayler, Pharoah Sanders, and John Tchicai. This tradition has lived on to the present day with subsequent waves of musicians like David Murray, David S. Ware, and Charles Gayle. Also, it should be noted that rock and roll owes a lot to Elvin Jones's drumming and Coltrane's energetic playing with multiphonics and overblowing. At this time in history, it is probably true that this part of Coltrane's legacy is held in as deep suspicion as is Miles's fusion legacy. Some critics, listeners, and musicians find the disciples lacking in comparison with their mentor to such an extent as to foment some resentment against Coltrane for inspiring them. Of course, it should be noted that there are musicians and fans who find this music to be art to live for and by.

Coltrane's "modal" and "energy" periods represent his most mature musical thought and practice. As such, the time of widespread understanding and acceptance of these aspects of his music is perhaps still in the future. However, like Miles, Trane has innovations he made before his most mature statements that, although held in suspicion at the time of their emergence, have already come to be universally accepted. Coltrane's earlier musical inventions have entered the common practice of mainstream jazz today, especially the harmonic substitutions he invented known as "Coltrane changes." "Giant

Steps" and "Countdown" are now standards in the contemporary jazz repertoire. More significant, Coltrane's approach to reharmonization (when the arranger writes new harmonies, new chords, to accompany the melody of a song or the improvisations of a song), modeled in such recordings as "Body and Soul" and "But Not for Me," is ubiquitous, making his harmonic thought part of the intellectual tradition of jazz writing and playing.

We should also note Coltrane's influence on the world beyond the United States and the world's influence on him. It is widely known that Trane was drawn to the musical traditions of India and parts of the continent of Africa. One might argue convincingly that Trane is one of the progenitors of what is now known as "world music." Though his explorations were not geared for pop consumption or even for the dance market, the globalization of African-based rhythms and the ubiquity of Afro-Latino rhythms are certainly part of his legacy. And of course there are his explorations of ragas and his interest in Ravi Shankar, who introduced many Westerners to the music of India. In the 1960s, many Americans shared Trane's interest in world musics and religions. Indeed, his spiritual seeking was in line with a larger cultural movement among those who sought an alternative to Christianity and an American way of life.

Miles was also greatly influenced by other musical traditions. He noted that with *Sketches of Spain,* he was especially inspired by Arabic chants and flamenco. Like a number of African American intellectuals and artists, including Langston Hughes, Richard Wright, Ralph Ellison, and Romare Bearden,

Miles found himself drawn to Spain and Spanish culture. At the encouragement of his wife, Frances, he went to see Roberto Iglesias's Spanish dancers, and he was drawn to flamenco, which reminded him of the blues.[1] It was also the Moorish influence that drew him deeper and deeper into Spanish history and culture. For Miles, the Arabic influence was also evident in jazz in Israel. (In typical Miles fashion, he asserted, "Arabs and Israelis get along all right, every day; it's the government that's fucked up!")

We have seen Davis's and Trane's influences upon each other as well as the role each played as artistic innovator. The third element of their legacy is the sound that continues to define the mainstream jazz combo in the twenty-first century. This is due partly to the force of Wynton Marsalis's celebrity (as he was and continues to be the most prominent face of classic jazz's resurgence during the 1980s and beyond) and his reliance upon Davis's approach to improvisation. Largely because of Marsalis and the school of musicians for whom he became the spokesperson, the sound of the Miles Davis Quintet is one of the foundational aesthetic models for the neo–hard bop movement. It should be noted that in the person of Wallace Roney, Miles inspired at least one other major trumpeter who, without the cultural agenda of the neoconservatives, followed his improvisational style. Marsalis's extraordinary musicianship was justly celebrated, especially since he came to prominence at a time when many young black instrumentalists were not interested in classic jazz as a career choice, having grown up in a world dominated by hip-hop. He caught the critics' ear as the voice of the future of jazz when, not yet out of his teens, he won Grammy Awards in both classical and jazz categories during the same year. And as if that were not enough, the young Marsalis not only was taking care of business on his horn, but was also an evangelist for the music and an indefatigable nurturer of young jazz talent throughout the country.

Marsalis's emergence also came with two features relevant to our discussion: a simultaneous embrace and rejection of Miles Davis. Davis was obviously one of the primary models for Marsalis's improvisational style *and* his fashion sensibility. The dress of performers is an important part of their reception and affects how people relate to them as artists. At the beginning of his national career, many of the articles written about Marsalis made almost obligatory reference to his Italian suits. His notoriety came at a time when many young black performers, spurred on by the failure of the local, state, and national government to support music programs in elementary schools, turned their backs on traditional musicianship, preferring electronics, sampling techniques, and beat boxing over knowledge of scales and harmony. Many of the popular artists also were brazenly rejecting mainstream dress and speech, screaming obscenities, and venting their desire to topple the prevailing order. In contrast, here was a young virtuoso, perfectly manicured, elegantly dressed in bourgeois fashion, and a passionate and eloquent speaker who never publicly resorted to using slang or Ebonics. Despite his bourgeois presentation, Wynton was not an Uncle Tom, but a throwback to the "race man" of the early twentieth century, replete with the politics of respectability. Historically, race men have been committed to the ideology of racial uplift. And as a race man, like nationalists of all stripes, he was very conservative and proclaimed a deep anxiety about preserving traditions. His initial presentation of these values looked a lot like that of the young Miles Davis. As we have seen, he was also elegantly dressed, proud of the tradition to which he belonged, outspoken, and dignified. While Marsalis might have had the greater command of the technical aspects of trumpet playing—as he was wont to point out in his public feuds with the elder Miles—he was in fact still playing out a version of Miles's ideas.

Even as he invoked early Miles in his music and dress, Wynton simultaneously rejected Miles's late styles of dress and music making. The jazz/rock fusion movement that Miles inspired was seen as partly responsible for the decline of acoustic jazz. Wynton was heralded as the savior of straight-ahead acoustic jazz. Defining himself as the anointed one because of his virtuosity, Marsalis carved out space for the jazz mainstream. He did so by publicly attacking the right (the popular fusion groups) and the left (the so-called avant-garde groups). Interestingly, he did not stop at excluding their music from the jazz canon; he also denigrated their modes of dress. So as Miles and others began to wear flowing robes and other non-Western designs rather than suits and sports coats, Marsalis dismissed them as a bunch of cats "wearing dresses."[2]

Davis's later quintet with Wayne Shorter (1964–1968) seems to be the most direct model for the playing styles of the first wave of young lions (many of the tenor players modeled themselves after Wayne Shorter, the pianists after Herbie Hancock, the drummers after Tony Williams, and so on), but they also emulated the Davis/Coltrane quintet.

Common wisdom has it that both Coltrane and Davis went on to make what is currently their most influential contributions to the art form during the 1960s, after the dissolution of the quintet. Yet the legacy of their collaboration from 1955 to 1961 is far-reaching. In certain quarters, it remains preeminent. For Roney, it is simply not possible to prefer the Wayne Shorter/Tony Williams band over the John Coltrane/Philly Joe Jones band because the members of the later band were playing extensions of the earlier band. You are always hearing the Coltrane/Davis collaboration, even when listening to the later band.

In the current scene, jazz styles are categorized in relationship to a putative common practice known as "mainstream." This mainstream designation is to a large extent the sound of the Miles Davis Quintet with John Coltrane. The sound of classic jazz as it is understood today features many of the characteristics that Miles made so appealing with his John Coltrane band. Mainstream jazz today is bebop-based, with the meshing of cool and hot styles that Miles popularized with his band. The preferred format is quintet—piano, bass, and drums rhythm section plus trumpet and saxophone on the front line. Despite the bebop lineup of the ensembles and the modern music approach to improvisation, "mainstream" jazz proficiency today connotes a great familiarity with "standards"— not necessarily the contrafactual melodies penned by bebop masters or the canonical compositions by recognized jazz composers (Duke and perhaps Monk are the exceptions), but the Tin Pan Alley hits favored by earlier generations of jazz musicians. Only Sonny Rollins rivals Miles in his ability to make classic instrumental jazz statements out of pre–World War II pop tunes. In today's scene, the ability to play these songs competently has become a sort of litmus test for inclusion in the ranks of the classic, mainstream jazz musicians.

The neo–hard bop movement, led by Wynton Marsalis, has brought jazz to heights of commercial, critical, and institutional support that far exceed any enjoyed by previous jazz musicians, including Trane and the Chief, the crown jewels of jazz's golden age. And in this way, the legacy of the Davis/Coltrane collaboration flourishes in the aesthetics of the current jazz scene.

As pervasive as their influence over contemporary jazz musicians is, Coltrane and Davis have a life beyond their music: Both are cultural icons. This is the fourth aspect of their legacy worth considering. Artists and political activists have mined both personas for inspiration and for examples of how to be in the world. Poets of the black arts movement effectively chose Coltrane as their patron saint. As artists who wanted their work to be relevant to what they saw as the black revolution, they considered Coltrane the new model of the aesthetic hero. He seemed to maintain the perfect balance of emotional intensity and intellectual depth. The visceral edge to his sound and the strength with which he played pointed both to genius in the conventional Western sense of that concept and to "the juju man" (one who works magic) in the African American sense. He was the possessor of a rarefied ability and understanding *and* a charismatic sound and projection.

People celebrated him because his music brought to mind the deepest concern for spiritual matters and the relentless drive for freedom and truth. Most of the biographies of Coltrane emphasize his spiritual focus to the exclusion of his interest in the contemporary and historical struggles of black people. Coltrane's spiritual focus is real and explicitly referenced by him, especially in his most popular recording, *A Love Supreme.* But there is no need to view these areas of concern as mutually exclusive or at odds with one another. According to his stepdaughter, Syeeda, *both* of her parents were keenly interested in the history and the plight of African Americans. They frequented bookstores and maintained a library at home that included sociological and historical literature as well as books about religion, philosophy, astrology, and mathematics. They heard Malcolm X give one of his eloquent speeches at a Harlem rally. Family discussions around the dinner table were more likely to touch upon the social movements of the time than arcane religious matters. As noted earlier, in Syeeda's words, "He loved his people."

Coltrane was among the first jazz musicians to name compositions in honor of his African heritage during the era of wars against colonialism, with tunes like "Tanganyika Strut," "Dahomey Dance," and "Liberia." Later, he also wrote the elegiac ballad "Alabama" in memory of the four black girls who died in a church bombing while worshipping in Sunday school. Reportedly, Coltrane based the melody upon the cadences in Reverend Martin Luther King Jr.'s sermon for the occasion.

Ultimately, Coltrane speaks to the poets of black liberation not so much because of his titles or even his public utterances, but more because of the sound and content of his music. With Trane, the ceremonial hipster is modified to take on aspects of revolutionary consciousness. He was not ranting against the system in a fashion that could be dismissed as ignorant. His was the musical intelligence of a person who had mastered the harmonic language and could play the expected conventions convincingly and with startling dexterity and freshness. His assault upon the diatonic system, then, was with the precision and care of someone who had learned to honor the various interrelations among the twelve tones but who could go beyond that system in a number of ways at will. So when Coltrane left the familiar world of European tonality, rhythm, and sound concepts, he entered the void with formidable navigating skills and the technique to follow through on his ideas. In Coltrane's music, one can hear the idea that as beautiful as life is, there is always a struggle for existence and ascension. So although he could sound like the destroyer of old forms, as Amiri Baraka would say, he never gave the impression that one had to simply rant against the system, fall into the abyss, or become nihilistic. His beauty and lyricism were earned, and not without strife and toil. However, he remained cognizant of the possibility and responsibility to build anew with more open values and love.

Miles is perhaps even more iconic than Coltrane. His persona is also more complex and lacks the relentless, monomaniacal approach to his goals that marked Coltrane's professional and personal lives. He appears to be riddled with contradictions and ironies. A part of his public reception is centered upon his sexuality, his coolness, his stature as the Chief, his ability and willingness to tell motherfuckers where to get off when they crossed the line. Baraka acknowledges the importance of this part of Miles's aura but also traces the music's development in line with the social reality that Miles the man inhabited. In one of the most provocative discussions of Miles's music during the 1950s and 1960s, Baraka sees Miles's band with Coltrane as the lead example of how jazz music became more than a retreat into coolness. Especially with Coltrane, the band's music had evolved to articulate the feelings and aspirations of black people.

> *In the postcool period Miles had begun to live hard in the ghetto, a condition particularly depressing because he was also addicted to heroin. From the drape-suited, gas-haired "cat," the Harlem music, particularly "Dig" and "Walkin'" and "Dr. Jackle," complete with Miles in pulled-down "black boy" hat and better-fitting Italian and Ivy threads, give Miles the "down" quality of the time.* Down, *the current parallel word for hip. Like Robert Thompson has said of Kongo culture, it prizes "getting down," bending the knees and elbows. It also favors "cool" as subtle fire. But now, too, the political sweep of the times meant one had to be down with the people, to be in touch with one's roots. The gospels and the blues were part of these roots. The music of this period is superbly funky and bluesy.*[3]

Baraka goes on to explain that Miles had serenaded his generation's youth as a cool bopper before his attitude and musical example joined the resistance against injustice that had taken center stage in the social movements of the mid-fifties. Pointing out how his generation grew up with Miles providing the hippest music for different periods, Baraka brings attention to another of the qualities that make Miles so intriguing: He was able to reinvent himself and his music several times. As he said to a condescending woman at a White House party during the Reagan years, "I've changed music five or six times." He came to New York a teenager, soon playing with the number one genius in the music. In the wake of Bird's death, Miles quickly became the number one bandleader. First as an acolyte and then as a leader, he played with the two most significant saxophonists *and* musical thinkers of the last half of the twentieth century. Sonny Fortune, who played alto and tenor saxophone with Davis, explained, "Miles had played with Bird. So Trane and everybody else knew that he knew something. And then he turned around and chose Trane after hearing and recognizing his importance. So Miles *had* to know something."

Trane led the way to the expressionism that gave life to the "new black aesthetic." The writers of the movement saw black music as the vanguard of the aesthetic. The black arts writers who came of age during Trane's artistic ascendancy adopted him as the leading voice of the music's new urgency and revolutionary fervor. Black culture in America always prized music as a transcendent voice for its aspirations—aspirations not easily or even safely coded in words. Indeed, at least from the times of the spirituals on, black musical expression has been the prime vehicle for expressing the very humanity of black folk. It was the spirituals that led those who heralded the first "new black aesthetic" a century ago, such as W. E. B. Du Bois and James Weldon Johnson, to point to black music not only as proof of black folk's humanity, but as the artistic basis of the soul of America. Two generations later, the vanguard musicians were still concerned with the soul of America, but this time revolution was in the air (rhetorically, at the very least). In his 1967 *Crisis of the Negro Intellectual,* cultural critic Harold Cruse praised jazz musicians as the most ambitious and important of the black intelligentsia, as they were imitated and followed by whites rather than the other way around.

The Miles/Coltrane band was a hallmark of the tradition set by the urban modern music movement led by Bird and others. The musical statements could be understood as an analogue of the resistance to oppression that culminated in the civil rights movement. This band modeled the principled stance of black people's march to a more democratic society. But with the black arts movement, the artistic challenge was to forge a new way, to create a more just and beautiful world, even if it meant a frightening annihilation of old forms. Coltrane's music took this important step; not content with democratizing the old order, he searched for "something that hasn't been played before." Music was more than a sonic representation of black life (as Duke Ellington would have it, for example); it was also a leading voice toward building something new. The challenge was to envision a culture and civilization *after* the apocalyptic violence that plagued America in the 1960s. As a bandleader, Coltrane was part of the search for both new skins and new wine. If the young writers of his day hailed the new music as the religion of the new black aesthetic, then Coltrane was its reigning prophet.

The fifth dimension of the legacy bequeathed to us by Coltrane and Davis centers on the ways they continue to inspire the artistic and spiritual life of our nation. Trane and the Chief remain relevant to American culture, and especially to African Americans, because they epitomize spirituality and coolness. In this case, spirituality is not tied specifically to religion. It is not a matter of chastity or ascetic ideals so much as it is of deep connection to life and an attempt to master the struggles that it involves. The spiritual life is built upon a commitment to truth telling and truth living. As master jazz musicians, Trane and the Chief presented their spirituality within the reality of cool.

Keep in mind that in many places within African America, "coolness," like "toughness" (in the sense of resilience without whining), is something rather like a moral category. Adopting the cool stance is one thing, but often it rings hollow, as though it is a collection of costumes and postures. Rather, what is revered is the person who *is* cool, who brings the virtues of this attribute to all of his or her undertakings. Being cool involves being relaxed, unruffled, quick-witted, reluctant to use aggression, and, most of all, able to follow one's own path. Coolness celebrates individuality.

With Miles we have the entire package. Yes, he had all of

the accoutrements and the mannerisms. But these were just the trappings, the surface (though important) stylings of a hip, cultural worker. The genuine article ultimately resided in his horn. With his instrument, he revealed his confident authority as he always, unhurriedly, told his story. His style of playing enabled him to make so much of so few materials, such as the way he could play one note and switch the direction or even the meaning of all that surrounded it.

At a deeper level, Miles the man, the thinking/acting person and not simply the musician, embodied the ideal of being cool. (Unfortunately, this coolness did not extend to his relationships with women, which could be quite abusive.) He was never cowed before racism or stupidity, he never engaged in false modesty to appear humble, and he never let anyone or anything diminish his self-worth. We think of the nineteen-year-old Miles who had the courage to turn his back on Fisk for Juilliard, who then turned his back on Juilliard for Bird. He was the black man in the 1950s driving a sports car, who lived and loved on his own terms and took a head whipping rather than bow and scrape under the power of racist New York cops. Miles was quintessentially cool.

After considering the myriad elements of the legacy bequeathed to us by Miles Davis and John Coltrane, it seems too easy to continue thinking of them only as the Prince of Darkness and the Bearer of Light, each occupying an opposing end of our spiritual and/or iconographic continuum. We would like to suggest a new way of looking at the two men: Ours is a vision inspired by elements of Yoruba-based religions. As the ways of the Yoruba religion have spread from Africa's Ile-Ife to Cuba, Bahia, New York City, and beyond, the god (called an orisha) Elegba has come to represent spirituality and coolness. Miles and Trane's collective example, as well as their individual biographies, suggests affinity with Elegba, the orisha of beginnings and transitions and the door to the pantheon of Yoruba deities. He is capricious and at times seems riddled with contradictions but ultimately lives beyond good and evil. Like Elegba, both of our musicians lived with constant change: Coltrane's music from one recording to the next often made him sound like several different artists, leaving audience members bewildered when confronting the difference between the Coltrane on their records and the live Coltrane in concerts. This drive to evolve and experiment went beyond the normal limits of professional musicians and was based firmly upon Coltrane's commitment to a God-centered, spirit-filled life. Similarly, Miles was able to change the surroundings of his band, providing ever fresh perspectives upon which to expound through his trumpet stylings. All access to the favors and consideration of other orishas must first begin by honoring Elegba, the orisha of the crossroads. Similarly, both Miles and Trane serve as stylistic and aesthetic guardians at the gates, between whom countless musicians have traveled toward their own attempts at freedom and self-expression. It might seem that it would take a composite of Coltrane and Davis to effectively call forth the energies of the two-faced trickster orisha, especially since Coltrane might be considered too fervent to legitimately be called cool and Miles too worldly to be considered spiritual. Nonetheless,

Miles certainly considered himself spiritual and found that music was his spiritual practice, connecting him to his predecessors Pops, Lady Day, Prez, Dizzy, Hank Jones, and others: "Music is some spiritual shit, man! If I do something, it's all in me, things I learned from all of them." And even Coltrane was cool, in the sense of being peaceful and calm. He is universally remembered as a man of few words, great humility, and general peacefulness, yet many accomplished poets understood his music as the probing search for ways to destroy the old order. Coltrane screamed and hollered in his music without it meaning anxiety and rage. When dubbed by critics as a "young angry tenor," Coltrane recoiled from this description, telling Frank Kofsky that he did not feel angry per se. Perhaps we cannot take Coltrane's words at face value here. But he always maintained a duality that seems akin to the duality of a trickster orisha. He maintained a sincere engagement with the cosmos and an equally deep serenity. Check out "Alabama," for example, which has both sides to it. He could be furious, though, as in his tour de force, "Chasin' the Trane," or, better yet, "Ascension," easily his most dissonant composition/performance. But he was equally beautiful and serene in compositions like "Dear Lord," "Naima," "After the Rain," and "Peace on Earth."

Trane, like Miles, was simply too complicated to be contained by any single category, emotion, or dimensional descriptor. These two men and the music they made together continue to provide us opportunity for greater exploration and understanding of their art and identities. They helped to shape and define the tenor of their times by always taking risks, by their willingness to stand at the edge of the abyss in order to expose the darkness below while simultaneously directing us to the light that exists just on its other side. In constant motion, continuous growth, these men and their music have much to teach us still.

Davis and Coltrane lived in a world where black people were daily confronted with demands for deference and submission to arbitrary, racist authority. Then, as now, the humanity, intelligence, beauty, and moral integrity of black folk were always held in suspicion. In this context, the two men engaged in an epic and heroic spiritual battle as they fought for dignity and for a world in which we can all be cool.

GLOSSARY

Altissimo the extreme high range of a horn. The altissimo register is above the normal range similar to the way the falsetto range is above the normal range of the singing voice.

Bar a "measure," as in written music.

Bebop an urbane and virtuosic form of modern jazz that began primarily in New York during the late 1930s and 1940s. The prime architects of its style include John Birks "Dizzy" Gillespie, Thelonious Monk, Kenny Clarke, Earl "Bud" Powell, and especially Charles "Bird" Parker.

Block Chords a style of playing melodies on the piano in which each note is accompanied by a chord, usually in tight voicing.

Bombs rhythmic accents made by the drummer that are unregulated and not part of the timekeeping scheme. During the bebop period, drummers began to follow Kenny Clarke's and Max Roach's lead in switching timekeeping function from the right foot to the right hand. The bass drum, no longer primarily a timekeeper, was used to "drop bombs" to spur the music and add intensity.

Bridge the second theme of a popular song form.

Burn to play with great intensity.

Change Running   playing something to delineate every chord in the song during a solo.

Chitlin Circuit   the aggregation of black-owned clubs and performing venues that catered to black audiences.

Chords   the harmonic underpinning of a song. A knowledge of chords and how to improvise using the harmonic sequence as a primary reference point became increasingly important after the advent of bebop.

Chorus   An entire rendition of a song's structure. In song forms that repeat, each repetition is said to be another chorus.

Chromatic   a movement from one note to the very next note recognized in the diatonic system.

Coloratura   a high-pitched operatic soprano voice that sings in an ornate style.

Common Time   see "four/four."

Comp   short for "accompany," it means to play the chords or harmonies of a song while another instrument or voice plays the melody or solos.

Contralto   a deep, low-pitched, resonant female voice.

Cool   a style of playing that is restrained and mainly lacking in the rhythmic and timbral intensity associated with "hot" music.

Cool Jazz   a style of jazz that retreated from the fast tempos and intensity of bebop music while retaining much of its syntax and vocabulary. It was associated primarily with white jazz musicians.

Cycle a harmonic progression that is repeated.

Date "record date"; a commercial recording session.

Diatonic the prevailing tonal system of Western civilization since the time of Bach, the *do re mi fa so la ti do* scale often taught in elementary schools.

Dorian the mode beginning on the second scale degree of the major scale.

Eighth Note rhythmic unit, usually worth one-half of the basic pulse, the general unit used for jazz solos after Charles Parker.

Four/Four metric system that obtains in most Western music, including popular music, in which there are four beats, or pulses, per measure. Also known as "common time."

Front Line the melody-playing instruments, as opposed to the instruments that make up the rhythm section.

Functional Harmony harmonic practices based upon the diatonic system.

Fusion jazz/rock fusion, a genre made popular by Miles Davis that featured electronic instruments and jazz solos over funky grooves based upon the conventions of rock or soul music.

Glissando a scalar passage played so fast as to approach sounding like a smear.

Half-Step the smallest melodic interval in the diatonic system.

Hard Bop   a style of music based upon bebop with gospel inflections. It was seen as a return to "black" values and practices in the music, partially in response to the phenomenon of cool jazz.

Harmony   the tonal accompaniment to a melody.

Hot   a style of playing that is characterized by rhythmic and timbral intensity.

Mixolydian   the mode beginning on the fifth scale degree of the major scale.

Modern Music   the name that the musicians chose for the music that eventually came to be known as bebop.

Motif   a melodic fragment or idea that is employed or developed.

Multiphonics   the practice of producing more than one note simultaneously on instruments designed to play only one note at a time, such as a saxophone.

Neo–Hard Bop   the style of generation X mainstream jazz musicians, modeled after the hard bop combos of the 1950s and 1960s.

New Thing   a name for the postbop, free jazz of the late 1960s. Important contributors to this style include Archie Shepp, the Art Ensemble of Chicago, Ornette Coleman, Cecil Taylor, and many others.

Octave   the interval between a note and its next repetition.

Ostinato   a melody, particularly in the bass line, that is repeated for a while.

Overblow   the practice of blowing in a horn in such a way as to produce tones that are in a higher register.

Pedal   a tone that is repeated or held for some time, especially in the bass line.

Rhythm Changes   the chord changes to "I Got Rhythm," used as the harmonic basis for hundreds of jazz compositions, second only to the blues in this regard.

Rhythm Section   the players in a band who function primarily to provide the rhythmic and harmonic accompaniment to a melodic statement or solo, usually the drums, bass, and piano/guitar.

Riff   a repeated, short, melodic motif, used rhythmically to accompany a melody or solo.

Rim Shot   a drum technique where the drum stick is struck against the metal rim of the drum rather than on the skin.

Scale   a collection of tones in consecutive formation.

Shout   a chorus of a song that features a riff-based alternate melody, usually preceding the final statement of the melody or the final chorus of a solo.

Solo   the improvised statement that a player makes over the harmonies of a song.

Straight Ahead   acoustic jazz that employs the classic practices of swing and improvisation in the manner of the bebop and hard bop masters.

Stroll   to "lay out," or stop playing while another player is soloing; used especially for pianists.

Suspension   the delay of a harmonic event.

Swing   a distinctive characteristic of jazz statement that has its roots in the African American synthesis of African and European rhythmic practices.

Third Stream   a music that sought to marry the stylistic ingredients of European art music with American jazz, the putative first and second streams, to produce a third stream. Its early enthusiasts included Gunther Schuller, John Lewis, and J. J. Johnson.

Time   when the drummer plays the traditional accompaniment, demarking the pulse and meter of the song, he or she is said to be "playing time."

Tonal   relating to the diatonic system of organization.

Tritone   the interval of a diminished fifth or augmented fourth. Bebop musicians were fond of substituting chords a tritone away from the expected chord to add harmonic interest in their compositions and improvisations.

ii-V-I   "two five one" progression, a commonly used harmonic progression that functions similarly to the IV-V-I progression in European art music. It is also used to describe melodic patterns that are used over this progression.

Unison   when two or more instruments or voices play the same note.

Up-Tempo fast-paced.

Vamp a repeated figure, a chord progression that is repeated indefinitely, or a bass figure that is repeated—for example funk music, especially that of James Brown, where the repeated bass lines and chords create a chantlike, hypnotic, and danceable sonic presence.

Voice Leading the practice of moving from one chord to the next with the least possible movement, especially when the motion resolves by a half-step.

Voicing the way that a chord is presented, the choice of notes, and their placement within the chord.

NOTES

Prelude: The Head

1. Carl Grubbs, conversation with authors, July 31, 2004, and Oliver Lake, e-mail correspondence with Farah Jasmine Griffin, July 6, 2005. See also Troupe Collection, interviews of Miles Davis. Schomburg Center for Research in Black Culture, New York Public Library, New York.

2. Stuart Elliot, "The Media Business: Advertising; Apple Endorses Some Achievers Who 'Think Different,'" *The New York Times,* August 3, 1998, late edition.

3. Oliver Lake, e-mail correspondence with Farah Jasmine Griffin, July 6, 2005.

4. Ben Ratliff, "Listening to CDs with Joshua Redman: Playing the Diplomatic Changes," *The New York Times,* May 27, 2005.

5. Joshua Redman, "A Love Supreme Interview with Joshua Redman," interview by Jerry Jazz Musician, December 12, 2001. See www .jerryjazzmusician.com (accessed February 5, 2008).

6. Michael Harper, quoted in John O'Brien, ed., *Interviews with Black Writers* (New York: Liverwright Publishing Corporation, 1973), 97–98.

7. Rashied Ali and Sonny Fortune, interview with authors, February 8, 2006.

8. Howard Johnson, interview by Salim Washington, August 4, 2004.

9. Amiri Baraka, conversation with authors, n.d.

Pass It On

1. Miles Davis with Quincy Troupe, *Miles: The Autobiography* (New York: Simon and Schuster, 1989), 28–29.
2. George Lipsitz, *A Life in the Struggle: Ivory Perry and the Culture of Opposition* (Philadephia: Temple University Press, 1988), 20.
3. Ibid., 23.
4. Ian Carr, *Miles Davis: The Definitive Biography* (New York: Thunders Mouth Press, 1998), 1.
5. The terrorism of the riots mobilized African Americans throughout the nation to protest against racial violence.
6. J. K. Chambers, *Milestones: The Music and Times of Miles Davis* (New York: Da Capo Press, 1998).
7. Davis and Troupe, 74.
8. Miles Davis never thought that fashion was as important as the music, telling Wallace Roney, "I'd let [the journalists] stick around, but all they wanna do is see what I got on."
9. See David Tegnell, "Hamlet: John Coltrane's Origins," in *Jazz Perspectives* (November 2007), 1, no. 2.
10. Syeeda Andrews, interview with authors, August 13, 2004.

The Birth of a New Freedom

1. John Szwed, *So What: The Life of Miles Davis* (New York: Simon and Schuster, 2002), 40.
2. Davis and Troupe, 58.
3. John Szwed, as reprinted in Leonard Feather, *The JAZZ Years: Earwitness to an Era* (New York: Da Capo Press, 1988), 91–93.
4. Szwed, 63.
5. Feather, 92.

6. Szwed, 64.

7. Davis and Troupe, 109.

8. We use the term "European art music" for what is popularly referred to as classical music. We shy away from this term as it is confusing because all cultures have classical expressions and even within the European tradition, classical music can refer to a specific period of its development after the Baroque period during the reign of Beethoven. The IV-V-I chord progression is codified in all of its flexibility by Bach so long ago and is the basis of virtually every single folk or popular song in the European and Euro-American musics until the blues. European "classical" music refers to a specific period in that musical tradition.

9. Eric Schneider, "Joints, Junk, and Jazz: The Transformation of Drug Culture in the 1940s," unpublished manuscript, 9.

10. Frank Kofsky, *Black Music, White Business: Illuminating the Political Economy of Jazz* (New York: Pathfinder Press, 1998), 39.

11. Szwed, 114.

12. Davis and Troupe, 188.

13. *TIME,* November 8, 1954.

14. Davis and Troupe, 188.

15. Davis and Troupe, 191.

16. Davis and Troupe, 192.

17. Davis and Troupe, 133.

18. Lewis Porter, *John Coltrane: His Life and Music* (Ann Arbor: University of Michigan Press, 1999), 36.

19. J. C. Thomas, *Coltrane: Chasin' the Trane* (New York: Da Capo Press, n.d., originally published 1975), 27.

20. Porter, 57.

21. John Coltrane, "Coltrane on Coltrane," *Down Beat* (September 1960), reprinted at www.downbeat.com (accessed February 5, 2008).

22. Ibid.

23. Porter, 90.

Struggle and Ascent

1. J. W. Milam and Roy Bryant later confessed to having murdered Till. The confession was published in *Look* magazine as "The Shocking Story of Approved Killing in Mississippi," June 1956.

2. Davis and Troupe, 197.

3. J. C. Thomas, 68.

4. Szwed, 122.

5. George Avakian, e-mail correspondence with Farah Jasmine Griffin, June 17, 2004.

6. George Avakian, *The Complete Columbia Recordings: Miles Davis & John Coltrane,* liner notes (Audio CD, May 4, 2004), 13.

7. Joyce Johnson, *Door Wide Open: A Beat Affair in Letters, 1957–1958* (New York: Viking, 2000), 41.

8. Davis and Troupe, 199.

9. *Saturday Review,* October 11, 1958.

10. In new research, historian Robin Kelley suggests that Art Blakey did not actually go to Africa although he claimed to have lived there for two years studying the music and cultures of West Africa.

11. Sy Johnson, communication with Salim Washington, n.d.

12. As quoted in Porter, 99.

13. Wallace Roney, interview with authors, July 2, 2007.

14. Troupe Collection.

15. Szwed, 145.

16. Davis and Troupe, 195.

17. Porter, 100.

18. Davis and Troupe, 212.

19. Syeeda Andrews, interview with authors, August 13, 2004.

20. Davis and Troupe, 207.

Interlude

1. Untitled review of Miles Davis Sextet at Newport Jazz Festival, Newport, July 1958, quoted in Ken Vail, *Miles' Diary: The Life of Miles Davis 1947–1961* (London: Sanctuary Publishing, 1997), 121.

2. *Down Beat,* June 1957. See Vail, 101.

3. Davis and Troupe, 199.

4. Zita Carno, "The Style of John Coltrane," *The Jazz Review,* October/November 1959.

5. Thomas, 95.

6. August Blume, "An Interview with John Coltrane," *The Jazz Review* (January 1959), 2, no. 1, 25.

7. Szwed, 141.

8. Davis and Troupe, 218.

9. Davis and Troupe, 216.

10. Wallace Roney, interview with authors, July 2, 2007.

Clawing at the Limits of Cool

1. Despite Smith's apparent lack of technical musical knowledge (he says that the title cut "will also stand out because it includes one of the most beautiful jobs on muted horn since Leon 'Bix' Beiderbecke, with a cornet and a piece of old felt, shook up the whole Whiteman band on Sweet Sue"), he was prescient in his understanding of this band's importance.

2. It is the second section, but also the middle because the form doesn't end after the second section, but always returns to the first section.

3. "The Music" is what jazz musicians call jazz.

4. "Caught in the Act: Miles Davis Sextet at Jazz Seville, Hollywood," in *Down Beat* (July 1959), 32.

5. CBS, Columbia's parent company, released Columbia recordings outside of the United States and Canada on the CBS label.

6. J. G. Weihing, letter to Teo Macero, February 24, 1961, Teo Macero Collection, Music Division, the New York Public Library for the Performing Arts, Astor, Lenox and Tilden Foundations. Macero response to Weihing, March 2, 1961.

7. Irving Townsend memo, Teo Macero Collection, November 8, 1960.

8. John Stubblefield, conversation with Salim Washington, September 12, 2004, and October 6, 2004.

The Tag

1. Davis and Troupe, 28–29.

2. Rafi Zabor and Vic Garbarini, "Wynton vs. Herbie: The Purist and the Cross-Breeder Duke It Out," *Musician Magazine,* March 1985.

3. Amiri Baraka, "Miles Davis: "One of the Great Mother Fuckers," in *The Music: Reflections on Jazz and Blues* (New York: William Morrow, 1987), 290–301.

BIBLIOGRAPHY

Baraka, Amiri. "Miles Davis: One of the Great Mother Fuckers." *The Music: Reflections on Jazz and Blues.* New York: William Morrow, 1987.

———. "The Screamers." In William J. Harris, ed., *The LeRoi Jones/Amiri Baraka Reader.* New York: Thunder's Mouth Press, 1991.

Carno, Zita. "The Style of John Coltrane." *The Jazz Review* 2, no. 9 (1959): 16–21; 2, no. 10 (1959): 13–21.

Carr, Ian. *Miles Davis: The Definitive Biography.* New York: Thunder's Mouth Press, 1988.

Chambers, Jack. *Milestones: The Music and Times of Miles Davis.* New York: Da Capo Press, 1998.

Cole, Bill. *John Coltrane.* New York: Da Capo Press, 1993.

———. *Miles Davis: The Early Years.* New York: Da Capo Press, 1994.

Crease, Stephanie. *Gil Evans: Out of the Cool, His Life and Music.* Chicago: A Cappella Books, 2002.

Davis, Gregory, and Les Sussman. *Dark Magus: The Jekyll and Hyde Life of Miles Davis.* San Francisco: Backbeat Books, 2006.

Davis, Miles, with Quincy Troupe. *Miles: The Autobiography.* New York: Simon & Schuster, 1989.

DeVeaux, Scott. *The Birth of Bebop: A Social and Musical History.* Berkeley and London: University of California Press, 1997.

Elliot, Stuart. "The Media Business: Advertising; Apple Endorses Some Achievers Who 'Think Different.'" *The New York Times,* August 3, 1998.

Feather, Leonard, and Miles Davis. "Blindfold Test." *Down Beat*: September 21, 1955; August 7, 1958; June 18, 1964; June 13, 1968; and June 27, 1968.

Feather, Leonard. *The JAZZ Years: Earwitness to an Era.* New York: Da Capo Press, 1988.

Fujioka, Yasuhiro, with Lewis Porter and Yoh-Ichi Hamada. "John Coltrane: A Discography and Musical Biography." In *Studies in Jazz,* vol. 20. Metuchen, N.J.: Scarecrow Press, Institute of Jazz Studies, Rutgers, the State University of New Jersey, 1995.

Gonzalez-Wippler, Migene. *Tales of the Orishas.* New York: Original Publications, 1985.

Johnson, Joyce. *Door Wide Open: A Beat Affair in Letters, 1957–1958.* New York: Viking, 2000.

Kahn, Ashley. *Kind of Blue: The Making of the Miles Davis Masterpiece.* New York: Da Capo Press, 2000.

Kelley, Robin D. G., and Earl Lewis. *To Make Our World Anew.* New York: Oxford University Press, 2000.

Kirchner, Bill, ed. *A Miles Davis Reader* (Smithsonian Readers in American Music). Washington, D.C.: Smithsonian Institution Press, 1997.

Kofsky, Frank. *Black Music, White Business: Illuminating the History and Political Economy of Jazz.* New York: Pathfinder Press, 1998.

Lipsitz, George. *A Life in the Struggle: Ivory Perry and the Culture of Opposition.* Philadelphia: Temple University Press, 1988.

Nisenson, Eric. *Ascension: John Coltrane and His Quest.* New York: St. Martin's Press, 1993.

———. *'Round About Midnight: A Portrait of Miles Davis.* New York: Da Capo Press, 1996.

Porter, Lewis. *John Coltrane: His Life and Music.* Ann Arbor: University of Michigan Press, 1999.

Ratliff, Ben. *Coltrane: The Story of a Sound.* New York: Farrar, Straus & Giroux, 2006.

———. "Listening to CD's with Joshua Redman: Playing the Diplomatic Changes." *The New York Times,* May 27, 2005.

Redman, Joshua. "A Love Supreme Interview with Joshua Redman." Accessed at www.jerryjazzmusician.com.

Szwed, John. *So What: The Life of Miles Davis.* New York: Simon & Schuster, 2002.

Tegnell, David. "Hamlet: John Coltrane's Origins." *Jazz Perspectives* 1, no. 2 (November 2007).

Thomas, J. C. *Coltrane: Chasin' the Trane.* New York: Da Capo Press, 1975.

Thompson, Robert Farris. *Flash of the Spirit: African & Afro-American Art & Philosophy.* New York: Vintage Books, 1984.

Vail, Ken. *Miles' Diary: The Life of Miles Davis, 1947–1961.* London: Sanctuary Publishing, 1997.

Von Eschen, Penny. *Satchmo Blows Up the World: Jazz Ambassadors Play the Cold War.* Cambridge: Harvard University Press, 2006.

Williams, Martin. *The Jazz Tradition.* 2nd ed. New York: Oxford University Press, 1993.

Williams, Richard. *The Man in the Green Shirt.* New York: Henry Holt & Co., 1993.

Zabor, Rafi, and Vic Garbarini. "Wynton vs. Herbie: The Purist and the Cross-Breeder Duke It Out." *Musician Magazine* (March 1985). In Robert Walser, ed., *Keeping Time: Readings in Jazz History.* New York: Oxford University Press, 1999.

DISCOGRAPHY

Blakey, Art, and the Jazz Messengers. *A Night at Birdland with the Art Blakey Quintet,* Blue Note BST 81522, 1956.

———. *A Night at Cafe Bohemia with the Jazz Messengers,* Blue Note BST 81507, 81508, 1973.

Brown, Clifford. *Clifford Brown and Max Roach,* EmArcy MG 26043, 1954.

———. *Clifford Brown and Max Roach at Basin Street,* Verve, 2002.

Brubeck, Dave. *Brubeck Time,* Columbia CL 622, 1955.

Coltrane, John. *Blue Train,* Blue Note BLP1577, 1957.

———. *Soultrane,* Prestige LP7142, 1958.

———. *Black Pearls,* Prestige LP7316, 1958.

———. *Giant Steps,* Atlantic 1311, 1959.

Davis, Miles. *The Complete Birth of the Cool,* Capitol CDP 94550.

———. *Dig,* Prestige 7012, 1951.

———. *'Round About Midnight,* Columbia CL 949, 1955.

———. *Relaxin' with the Miles Davis Quintet,* Prestige 7129, 1956.

———. *Steamin' with the Miles Davis Quintet,* Prestige 7200, 1956.

———. *Workin' with the Miles Davis Quintet,* Prestige 7166, 1956.

———. *Cookin' with the Miles Davis Quintet,* Prestige 7094, 1956.

———. *Miles Ahead,* Columbia CL 1041, 1957.

———. *Milestones,* Columbia CL 1193, 1957.

————. *Miles Davis at Newport 1958,* Columbia CL 2178, 1958.

————. *Kind of Blue,* Columbia CL 1355, 1959.

————. *Sketches of Spain,* Columbia CL 1480, 1959.

————. *Someday My Prince Will Come,* Columbia CL 1656, 1961.

————. *Miles Davis & John Coltrane, The Complete Columbia Recordings, 1955–61,* Columbia C6K65833.

————. *In Stockholm 1960 Complete,* Dragon DRCD 228.

Eckstine, Billy. *Billy Eckstine and His Orchestra, 1944–1945,* Classics 914, 1996.

————. *Billy Eckstine and His Orchestra, 1946–1947,* SDA 16096, 1998.

Jackson, Milt. *MJQ,* Prestige OJC-125, 1955–1961.

Monk, Thelonious. *Thelonious Monk Quartet with John Coltrane at Carnegie Hall,* Blue Note 0946 35173 2 5, 2005.

Parker, Charlie. *The Complete Savoy and Dial Studio Recordings,* Savoy 92911-2, 1945–1948.

Roach, Max. *The Best of Max Roach & Clifford Brown in Concert,* Crescendo GNP S18, 1980.

ACKNOWLEDGMENTS

A number of generous and insightful individuals have offered assistance and advice to us throughout the course of researching and writing this book. To them we are eternally grateful. Sean Desmond was the project's original editor. In fact, he approached us with the idea for a book about Miles Davis's Prestige recordings with John Coltrane. Sean always saw the book's potential, and his patience and careful reading of various versions of the manuscript helped us tremendously. Peter Joseph inherited the book from Sean, and we couldn't have wished for a more enthusiastic, engaged reader. Peter is a gifted editor, and we are honored to have worked so closely with him. The finished project has benefited greatly from his tireless efforts, his patience, and his multiple readings.

We have been very fortunate to interview people who knew and/or worked with Miles Davis and John Coltrane, people who saw the various incarnations of Miles's band in the late fifties, and a number of people who have been students of their music. Among these we want to thank Carl Grubbs, Rashied Ali, Sonny Fortune, Wallace Roney, Jimmy Cobb, John Stubblefield, Howard Johnson, Oliver Lake, George Avakian, George Stade, and Chuck Stewart. Not only has Mr. Stewart's long career of documenting our most important artists yielded an exquisite photographic record, but he is a walking archive for anyone who wants to learn about the music and its makers. Coltrane's stepdaughter, Syeeda Andrews gave us one of our most memorable and inspiring interviews. Wallace Roney, a musical genius in the tradition of Miles Davis, is not only a master musician, but also an astute historian of the music. Over a long dinner in Greenwich Village, Stanley Crouch shared his wisdom, his vast knowledge of the music, and his sense of the importance of the American South to both musicians. In so doing, he helped give grounding to the project. Throughout, Amiri Baraka has been a guiding inspiration. We even paraphrased one of his lines of poetry for the book's title. And over an impromptu cup of coffee one spring afternoon in New York (where Morningside Heights merges with Harlem), he generously shared his brilliant analysis and his storehouse of knowledge about Miles, Trane, and the music. These two men, Stanley Crouch and Amiri Baraka, are among our greatest resources about U.S. history and culture and about this music we call jazz and its global significance.

Scholars such as Eric Schneider, Robin D. G. Kelley, John Szwed, Krin Gabbard, Maxine Gordon, Lewis Porter Thomas Doughton, Brent Hayes Edwards, Guthrie Ramsey, Anthony Monteiro, George Lewis, David Tegnell, and Robert G. O'Meally shared their own groundbreaking research, provided leads on where to track down recordings, clips, obscure articles, and interviews, and, in the case of Maxine, even intervened in our behalf. John Szwed not only shared his research, he also read the manuscript as well. He is our sage. Robin, Robin, Robin—our guardian angel and ideal reader. Quincy Troupe donated his taped interviews with Miles Davis to the Schomburg Center. It is a wonderful resource. Diana Lachatanere, head archivist, Manuscripts, Archives, and Rare Books, provided access to this treasure.

Geri Allen, Cheryll Greene, Ellie Hisama, Fred Ho, Jack Surridge, Anders Stefansen, and others provided stories, analyses, opportunities to share our work, and ears for listening. We also wish to express our gratitude to Loretta Barrett, of Loretta Barrett Books Literary Agency. Sharon Harris of the Institute for Research in African American Studies at Columbia University helped to track down much needed permissions; she has a magic touch for doing so. Research assistants Patricia Laspinasse and Alexis Charles were vital to the project. Wilhelmena Griffin lived through the times and listened to the music at its incarnation. The music of Miles and Trane is the music of her generation. She gave us a sense of its immediacy and loved and nurtured us as we tried to bring it to life.

We also wish to express our appreciation to the following very important institutions: the Troupe Collection at the Schomburg Center for Research in Black Culture; the Teo Macero Collection; the Music Division of the New York Public Library for the Performing Arts; the Astor, Lenox, and Tilden Foundations; the Institute for Jazz Studies at Rutgers University and its wonderful staff; the Institute for Studies in American Music at Brooklyn College; the Institute for Research in African American Studies and the Center for Jazz

Studies, both at Columbia University; the Dorothy & Lewis B. Cullman Center for Scholars and Writers at the New York Public Library.

Finally, we save our biggest thank-you for last: to Miles Davis and John Coltrane.

INDEX

Minton's, 68
Mitchell, Roscoe, 241
"Moanin'", 91
Mobley, Hank, 220
modal jazz, 177–79, 183, 194–95,
    230, 239–41
Modern Jazz Quartet (MJQ), 80, 87,
    121, 123
"Moment's Notice," 160–62
Monk, T. S. (Thelonious's son), 168
Monk, Thelonious
    at Carnegie Hall, 168–69
    with Coltrane, 11, 149, 159,
        163–66, 180–81, 229
    compositions, Davis's recordings
        of, 65, 89, 199, 203
    composition style, 163–64
    with Davis, 62, 68–70, 89–90
    at Five Spot, 166–68, 180–81
    innovations, 70, 162
    at Minton's, 68
    at Newport Jazz Festival, 93
    Prestige recordings, 85
    with Rouse, 135
    style and technique, 69–70, 162,
        163–65, 166
    virtuosity, 24
"Monk's Mood," 163
"Moody's Mood for Love," 65
"Moose the Mooche," 68
Morgan, Lee, 100, 160, 162
Morrison, Toni, 29, 30–31
Morrow, George, 124
Morton, Jelly Roll, 30, 178, 225
Mulligan, Gerry, 75, 77, 83, 93,
    173
Murray, Albert, 11, 64
Murray, David, 242
"My Favorite Things," 195
"My Funny Valentine," 89

"Naima," 115, 257
Nance, Ray, 73
Navarro, Fats, 66, 97, 116, 124
Newport Jazz Festival, 93, 121, 202
Norvo, Red, 73
"Now's the Time," 62, 63–65, 93, 200
"Nuit sur les Champs-Élysées," 177

Oliver, Jimmy, 100
Oliver, King, 131
"Oomba," 127

Page, Hot Lips, 81
Page, Walter, 134
Painter, Nell, 32
"Pannonica," 164
Paris, Davis in, 81–83, 170, 179–80
Parker, Charles "Bird"
    Adderley and, 94, 187
    "Billie's Bounce," 62
    blues style, 92
    with Coltrane, 101
    with Davis, 20–21, 44, 59, 61–62,
        66, 67–68, 74–75
    death, 109–10, 164
    drug addiction, 74–75, 83, 84
    in Eckstine's band, 45
    Gillespie, one-upmanship with,
        20–21
    in Hines's orchestra, 60–61
    improvisation, 65
    innovations, 91, 232
    at Minton's, 68
    musical influence and significance
        of, 1, 110, 237
    at Paris Jazz Festival, 81
    in Philadelphia, 102
    quintet format, 21–22
    at Royal Roost, 76
    variety of jazz forms, 64